FINDING COMFORT IN MY OWN SKIN:

MY JOURNEY IN SELF-PRESERVATION

Tamara M. Burnett

ISBN-13: 978-0692570593
ISBN-10: 0692570594

Dedication

This book is dedicated to everyone who has ever been unsure of or doubted your reason for existing. Know that there is a place and a purpose for you and never allow anyone to tell you different.

To my children, everything I strive to be in life is rooted in the love I have for you.

CONTENTS

Tamara M. Burnett

Tamara M. Burnett

Happiness is....

Loving Yourself

FOREWORD

When I began this book-writing journey, I had an abundance of ideas that came and went, (*mostly went*), because I was thinking so hard about the content and the many ways I could say one word, or describe a particular subject or moment. I wanted to present the very best book possible and as I sat and typed it became difficult to move along. I was literally a prisoner of my own thoughts, each one deeper than the previous, with no end in sight, like spinning on the proverbial hamster wheel. Growing up, I was usually the one who thought everything through so while this was not a surprise to me, I was unable to move forward. Why am I stuck? (*I thought*). What's holding me back? One day it became all too clear to me. I was overthinking. Why is this a bad thing? Well, it is not necessarily a bad thing but in the context of book writing, it was stifling. I realized I was overthinking because I wanted my book to be perfect, yet I wanted it to speak from my heart. There lies the problem. Perfection and my reality cannot coexist. No one is perfect. This revelation took me back to my teenaged years when although I was an intelligent, level headed, individual, I was often a dramatic over-thinker.

Fortunately, it was not to my detriment thanks to a series of self-esteem boosting situations in my life which forced me to concede things aren't always as bad as we make them. Everything negative that happens to you doesn't always require a response, nor does it require you to stay there. Understanding and applying this concept to my life has made a world of difference in not only how I view myself, and others, but in how I view the teachable moment that is almost always present. Why be a prisoner of the moment, your mind, or the minds of others? Seize the moment and press on. Sure it's a lot easier to say than do but once you get the hang of it, you will be free indeed. Free to live, love, laugh and learn, without fear of judgment, ridicule, peer pressure, or rejection. Freedom to make your own decisions and live with them, freedom to say no to feelings of insecurity and actually mean it, freedom to not care what others think of you while finally coming to the realization that you control your own destiny. Many of our insecurities and weaknesses are rooted in leaning too much on what people will think and say about us, when in the grand scheme of things, all that truly matters is our belief in self. One of the greatest mistakes we can make as human beings is allowing opinions and actions of others to have power over our lives. Ironically, the same individuals whom we allow to permeate our minds with self-doubt are just as broken and discouraged in their own existence.

In other words, MISERY DEMANDS COMPANY. However, you can refuse to join the party. Don't participate in the deconstructing of your mind, soul, and spirit, but be encouraged by the potential that is within you. Surround yourself with people who use their voice to speak life into others instead of those who use their voice to ridicule, destroy, demean, judge and belittle. You ultimately have power over yourself, and when you truly begin to recognize this as a fact, you will soar to a place of comfort in your own skin, and confidence in your abilities.

INTRODUCTION

As a young girl, I often struggled with fighting to be me and the perception of others that I was stuck-up, snobby, stand-offish, mean, and conceited, when the simple answer is, I was learning how to love myself. It had nothing to do with who they were but everything to do with who I was and strived to be. I was literally under construction. During construction, it takes time to build a proper foundation to ensure the frame will not collapse, and in this manner, I was in the process of being molded by God for a purpose. A purpose bigger than anyone's perception of me and although I was too young to realize it, God taught me to preserve myself until my purpose was revealed.

Looking back on the people and circumstances that sought to derail me from my purpose, made me realize how much value we, as a society, place on meaningless things. We exalt individuals for beauty, sexuality, status, abilities, money, among other things, yet we forget the importance of first being decent human beings. I was raised in a single-parent home and my mother is one of the best people anyone can ever meet. She exemplified class, beauty, strength, determination, struggle, and still found time to smile. She was usually happy and showed my brother and me how to be decent human beings who treat people the way we want to be treated. I remember watching how she interacted with people from all walks of life, the way she genuinely smiled at those she encountered, and even held conversations as if she knew them. From the pizza guy, to the grocery store clerk, and on to the homeless person on the street, they were all the same in her eyes. As I grew older, it never changed.

Watching my mother had a huge impact on the way I

view people and it also taught me that I am no better than the next person, just as they are no better than me. This way of thinking is what ingrained in me a strong sense of self that I believe is indestructible. I recognize your value, just as I recognize my own, which allows me to live life on my terms. Even in the awkward and unsure phase of my life, I never wanted to be anyone else, only my best self. I would become frustrated over what I thought were shortcomings I had control over but for some reason could not conquer. Little did I know, it was a part of my process, a process I actually had no control over, which shaped me into the person I am today. I am strong, yet sensitive. I am firm, yet sincere. I am positive, yet realistic. I am a leader, yet not afraid of following. I am a talker, yet I make it a point to listen. I am imperfect in many ways, but my imperfections are what make me great. I wholeheartedly accept that I am imperfect and it is my goal to help others do the same.

We need more authentic role models in society today to help children navigate a world where bullies can hide behind a computer, where body shaming is prevalent, where social media is the way to "fit in", where fake body parts are heralded as natural beauty, where taking the perfect selfie is more important than actually loving the person in the picture, and finally where more concern is placed on giving a false perception than embracing the truth. The problem is, adults are dealing with some of the same issues of self-acceptance that make it difficult to exist without validation. Make no mistake about it; the need for validation is a dangerous state of being that embodies a people pleasing mentality, one that will never be at peace. This book is written with the intent of empowering individuals beyond the need for validation.

To demonstrate the power you have over your reactions to every situation that confronts you and to become fulfilled in the concept of self-actualization is to live.

In this book, I take you on my journey to self-actualization. A journey riddled with instances that could have derailed me but only helped me realize my power, a journey where I learned to be comfortable in my own skin. Do what you genuinely feel is best for you, don't seek validation, love the skin you're in, trust your instincts, stand up for yourself, love those who love you back, ignore those who mean you no good, find happiness in the small things, and live to find and fulfill your purpose.

1 THE COCOON

First the particulars: Tamara Marie Fleming, a shy, fun-loving, intelligent, strong-willed, and stubborn young girl to be exact. Never willingly played second fiddle yet not quite confident enough to take first. Why? Several reasons as you will soon find out, none of which matter anymore but for the purpose of this book, however, if this sounds familiar to you, commitment to change and embracing your purpose will remedy this ailment.

Growing up a shy girl limited me in ways I only truly acknowledged recently and it is this acknowledgment that was the catalyst for my drastic change in attitude. For example, I was blessed with many gifts: singing, dancing, poetry and song writing, yet there are many people in my life who are fairly close to me who would never know. Why? I was always too shy to express myself publicly using these platforms. Where did this shyness come from? I believe a number of factors played a role in this and to be frank, parental roles and environmental interpretation are high on the flowchart.

To be clear, parents' play an essential role in how well children will respond to stress, judgment, peers, change, and life in general, so for all parents' reading this, take careful consideration. Encourage your children through their deficiencies to cultivate a spirit of confidence (YES I CAN!) and perseverance (YES I WILL!) in all they aspire to be. In referencing my lack of expanding on the many talents I possess, at one point I became frustrated. Frustrated because I am a champion of self-esteem and self-efficacy, yet somehow this did not translate to sharing or expressing myself through talents and gifts. I am still a bit confused by this contradictory manner in which I existed but hey it was all a part of the process.

I recall being a shy little girl with so much to say, one who would pick and choose when and where to say it. In some ways, this is a sign of wisdom, one could surmise, but for me it was a bit more complicated. You see, I am a thinker, my analytical prowess often times representing more than the average person would deem relevant, however, in my mind, it was very necessary. Depending on who you asked, my grandmother for example, I just liked to hear myself talk, even as a toddler and into my formative years. My grandmother once told me a story about how she used to ask me to play a game of silence for five minutes at a time due to my constant chatter. I would never make it, my mind so full of thoughts and ideas that needed to be shared with whomever would listen. Just the thought of keeping what I considered to be hot topics and ideas to myself made me want to explode, literally. Strangely, this passion never translated into my artistic talents and gifts, however, as you read this, I have worked on it. I could go on forever about what I believe is the root cause for this but in relation to what I stated before, it's complicated. Nevertheless, I am who I am, and if I could change anything about my childhood, it would have been to experience mental and spiritual freedom. Freedom to not only passionately express my point of views but freedom of artistic and social expression, filtered yet without inhibition. Freedom of not caring about people watching me, judging me, criticizing me, mocking me, thinking less of me, although none of this should matter, it did.

Now my goal in life is to help my children and many others in the world who struggle with this, reach a point where none of it matters. I never want to see another person, man, woman, boy or girl, allow life's opportunities to linger or pass by for fear of what people say and think. One of life's greatest tragedies is unfulfilled potential and I am inspired to do everything in my power to avoid this fate.

Growing up without the presence of a father had already shaped me in ways I could not explain especially because during this time, I had no reason to believe I was negatively affected. I just lived the life I was given with the hopes of somehow coming out victorious in the end. It never occurred to me that my thoughts, words, and actions were that of a fatherless child protecting myself from the unknown. Moving away from familiar surroundings added to this fear of the unknown so I created a wall to protect myself from it, (*whatever "it" was*).

Today, it is difficult for me to dwell on my fatherless childhood, but I must acknowledge the role it played in shaping my mentality, my experiences, and life in general, something I previously failed to recognize. I believe the move to Sacramento occurred just in time to see me through the end of my formative years. My difficulty with moving stemmed from the drastic change of scenery while I was in the process of discovering my true identity. This type of change happens every day to children around the world and is in many ways a character building process. I had no concept of this back then, but the move also forced me to learn to adjust to new environments and was representative of the flexibility that would be necessary in the real world.

My journey, similar to many others, was a sink or swim process where although I had no control over the move, I could force the outcome in my favor. As I stated before, I was being molded and shaped for a purpose that did not become clear right away because I needed to experience life outside of my comfort zone. I had to be separated from everything I knew and all that was comfortable to me, and this is exactly what happened. A new city, new school, new neighborhood, new friends, and a new life, it was all a bit overwhelming at first and it didn't help that I refused to acknowledge my new home, I saw it as a temporary arrangement. This way of thinking contributed to my anxious and shy disposition, which initially prevented me from seeing the positive aspects of my situation.

My mother was aware of my silent protest but in her humble opinion, she was doing what was best for my brother and me, and moving back to Oakland was non-negotiable. In other words, I needed to get over it. I remember her telling me not to worry about anything, and everything would be fine once I met new friends. Her tone very unassuming yet reassuring leading me to a place of realizing this was my new reality. Although, the rebel in me still wanted to fight it, clearly this was a battle I would not win. Here is where I learned the concept that change is constant and oftentimes necessary, even when it doesn't feel good.

2 NECESSARY CHANGE

One of the most significant events of my life occurred in the summer of 1987. My mother decided to move from Oakland, California to Sacramento, California. Although I did not realize it at the time, this was the best move she could have made for my brother and me. It took a few months for me to understand the true significance of the move and how it would benefit me in the future but I could not imagine how I would ever begin to love this place when my heart and soul were in Oakland. Even when we officially moved to Sacramento, I made my way back to Oakland every chance I could get. By train, by bus, by car, it made no difference. I probably would have ridden my bike back home if necessary to get away from what I viewed as a hot and boring place to exist. Everything and everyone I knew was in Oakland, (*why would she do this to us?*), I asked over and over if we could move back but my Mother never wavered.

Today I can truly say I am grateful for the move, I met my wonderful sister-friends, and the adoring man I would eventually marry, but as a thirteen-year old trying to find her way, it was difficult. I must admit, even with the difficulties, my path always seemed to be scattered with a fair share of rainbows. Did I see them as rainbows then? I will not lie and say I did, but somehow I could always see the bright side of everything. My sunny yet shy disposition on display most times as I was conflicted about who I thought I was and the purpose of my existence.

I possessed the uncanny ability to be relatable when I felt the need to, but cautiously guarded as a means of survival. When I think about it, I was far too young to be this insightful, and as I later found out, it was more than necessary. If not for my high-level thinking outside the box, Lord knows where I would be today. Would I have preferred to have the carefree childlike enthusiasm of Riley Curry? Sure, and I have no doubt my life would look quite different if that were the case, but that is not my journey. My journey consisted of masked uncertainty and quiet confidence, a journey that although many can relate, they will fail to acknowledge. My journey from Oakland to Sacramento, being thrust into an unfamiliar setting was precisely what I needed and but for this journey, I would not be complete.

3 THE METAMORPHOSIS

It was the first day of school that I dreaded in my new surroundings, I remember like it was yesterday. I was a bit anxious to get the day over with, yet hesitant to open up and make new friends. I was an introvert by nature so introducing myself to people I may or may not remember a week from now, did not interest me in the least, especially in my new city of Sacramento. Everything was drastically different from what I was used to in Oakland: people, weather, neighborhoods, and even the bus system. There were times when the bus wait would last up to an hour or more on top of the hundred degree days that seemed to go on forever and ever. Needless to say, I was not happy.

Adding insult to injury, weeks before school started, my brother contracted the Chicken Pox and I eventually contracted them as well. The worst part is the disease spread all over my face and body just in time for the first day of school. Meeting new people with black marks all over my face was definitely not an ideal start to a new beginning. In every class I remained tight-lipped and observant with thoughts of how I could force my way back to Oakland. I recall getting lots of stares, not sure if it was because I was new or all the black marks on my face, I chose to believe the latter which gave me even more reason to be quiet. (*Just so you know, vanity was also a struggle of mine*). In Oakland, I always had a cute face and flawless skin. My Aunt NeNe used to tell me to take care of it, so imagine my disappointment when upon arriving to the first day of a new social life, my flawless skin was now flawed. (*How could I make a fabulous first impression like this?*) In my opinion, I could not. However, much to my surprise, someone saw the beauty beyond the scars and was not shy about letting me know.

It was the last class of my first day: Eighth period P.E. I walked into the gym alone and was ushered to the bleachers where I waited for my name and number to be called. I quickly sat on the first or second row in order not to bring much attention to myself. As I sat and waited, more students filed into class, some barely beating the bell, others just blatantly tardy. I tried not to make eye contact with anyone for fear of appearing to be either a) interested in them, or b) want to make new friends. As I stated before, I wanted neither, I just wanted to go home.

The more we sat, the more restless the class became. There was chatter coming from almost every bench, which was quickly drowned out by the loud and boisterous rapping of LL Cool J's song, *I'm Bad*. I quickly turned around to see where it was coming from then a combination of a smirk and a frown flashed across my face, astonished at how bold this boy was. He literally rapped the song from beginning to end, word for word, lyric for lyric, as loud as he possibly could I thought, (*with no music mind you*), and the P. E. teacher said nothing. I wanted to turn around and tell him to "Sit down and shut up!" but a part of me wanted to roll on the floor with laughter. Still, another part of me wished I were that bold and carefree. It was as if he was the only person in the room and no one or nothing else mattered. I soon convinced myself he was getting on my nerves even though I secretly wanted to join in. I was a huge fan of LL Cool J and this was one of my favorite songs and just like my classmate, I knew every lyric.

After he finished his performance, it was time for us all to go sit on the numbers we were assigned and this number is where we would sit everyday for the entire school year. My number turned out to be right next to Little Rapper Boy, (*how lucky for me*). Almost immediately he began talking my ear off just as he had almost rapped it off earlier in the same loud, boisterous tone. He asked me every question imaginable as if he were interviewing me for an open job position. He even asked me about "all the black spots" on my face, (*the nerve of him!*). Talking about the spots in a lighthearted manner made them seem less significant and just for good measure, Little Rapper Boy said I was still cute. I wasn't sure if I should be flattered or annoyed at his backhanded compliment but it did make me view the black spots differently.

Still, he asked more questions, I hesitated to answer them but deep down, I liked the attention. He was tall, dark, and full of humor. He even laughed at his own jokes. Admittedly he was very funny and actually made what started out as a mediocre day, a relatively enjoyable one. I never told him that but the huge Kool-Aid smile he wore everyday he sat next to me, told me had an idea. At this point, nothing could replace Oakland but meeting people like Little Rapper Boy on my first day, chipped away at the self-made cocoon I constructed, making it a little easier for me to be open-minded to the idea of making new friends. In his own way, he demonstrated for me a strong sense of self I secretly admired, no matter how annoying.

4 THE MESSAGE

Although I had every reason to have a bad day, it actually turned out to be a great start to new beginnings. My new school was really not as bad as I had drummed up in my mind. From this point on I decided to give my new life a chance, (*as if I had a choice anyway*) and besides, Oakland was still only a quick train or bus ride away (*since my mom refused to take me every weekend*).

Today, I appreciate my mom for not giving in to my selfish desires and doing what she felt was necessary as a parent. Teenagers are in no position to make rational, carefully thought-out decisions and even though I knew I had all the answers, I soon learned that mother knew best. In addition to not giving in, my mother allowed me to vent, within reason. She would check in with me, asking for my opinion of our new surroundings and if I uttered a negative word, I would be diverted back to reality with a simple message, "you will be fine." She never coddled me and acted as if she felt sorry for me (*that would have made things worse*), but encouraged me through words and deeds to see the bright side of the situation. Now it makes sense how a woman in her mid-sixties looks so young and usually wears a smile, in her world, there is little reason to do otherwise.

Watching my mom choose positivity in spite of her circumstances had a huge impact on me and became just what I needed to get through the transition of moving to Sacramento. I believe her rosy disposition carried me through the first day of eighth-grade and although I did not want to be there, I was able to find a silver lining in the clouds. That silver lining came in the form of a loud-mouthed, carefree young boy who demonstrated for me that life is what you make it, and doesn't always have to be so serious. In one fifty-minute block of time, I learned to relax, live a little (*just a little*), and that even with black marks on my face, my true beauty shined through. Lessons that revealed to me a glimpse of sunshine from the tunnel I unknowingly created.

5 DECISIONS

As I adjusted to my new school and living arrangements I still felt the pull of the city I loved. Every weekend, holiday, spring and summer break, I found a way to get back there. Although I began to make new friends, somehow it wasn't enough. I daydreamed about one day moving back home but as time passed on, it became apparent that at the very least, Sacramento would be home until I became old enough to move back to Oakland on my own, so I might as well make the best of it.

The beginning of my eighth grade year was a blur aside from my encounter with Little Rapper Boy, but that soon changed when I noticed a certain someone who, to my surprise, noticed me too. In the interest of being completely transparent, I may have never known he was interested if it were not for whom I thought was a messy, meddling, classmate who was friends with him and merely acquainted with me. I am certain I would have never divulged my interest to this person whom I will affectionately name, Cool Dude, not because I thought he was cool but because he clearly thought so himself.

Although I liked him, I was too shy to show interest publicly and even privately, as you will soon find out. I would ignore him in class, at lunch, on the way home, basically everywhere. Today I can admit I was afraid to show interest because I was afraid of where it might lead, some place I was not ready to go. Can't I just like him from a distance? That seemed perfectly okay with me, until the messy meddling acquaintance decided to help us connect. I recall walking between classes one day, minding my business when I was interrupted by a loud, boisterous voice yelling my name. At first I planned to ignore it but chose to make the noise stop instead by acknowledging its existence. No sooner than I turned towards the yelling of my name did I see the messy, meddling classmate walking with Cool Dude, waving frantically while flashing a mischievous grin. She knew I liked Cool Dude and he liked me so she wanted me to see her walking with him, I immediately thought, *(how rude)*.

Add this reason to the long list of why I wanted to go back home. Obviously, none of my friends in Oakland would act this way. I obliged and waved, peering at the awkward moment Messy Girl created. Cool Dude clearly not a willing participant but nonetheless he smiled and gave a nervous nod, seemingly taken aback by the moment, which was completely understandable. What now? All I could think about is how awkward our next classroom encounter would be, I actually preferred the mystique of knowing we had eyes for one another without the interaction. Sounds strange huh? Remember, I was only thirteen years old and believe it or not, I was right where I needed to be, in the shy, awkward, uncertainty phase. Little did I know, things were about to get even more strange.

The next morning as I prepared for school, I wondered what Messy Girl would do for an encore. I was convinced she had a vendetta against me and wanted Cool Dude for herself and her antics the day before were only the beginning. My walk to school did not last long enough; I reached the doors of the school hallway seemingly quicker than usual so I slowed my pace a bit, peering around every corner trying to avoid the inevitable. It was only a smile and a wave and I had somehow turned it into a made for T.V. drama, *(but isn't that what teenaged girls do?*) Instead of focusing on my next class, I was caught up in what would happen next with Cool Dude. In due time, my questions were finally answered during first lunch period when Cool Dude approached me and asked for my number. This was it, the moment I secretly waited for and dreaded at the same time. I was nervously cool, if that makes any sense, if it doesn't, just know that I was shaking inside but calm and collected on the outside. It was only a boy, what's the big deal? If only I had that mindset then. I scribbled my name and number on his notebook and he scribbled his on mine. Now what? He said he would call later that evening and for the sake of not appearing to be desperate I smiled and quickly walked away with my heart pounding as if it were going to explode.

The last two classes on my schedule might as well have been cancelled. I spent the next few hours of my life daydreaming about Cool Dude asking me for my number and what I would say when he called, too much time wasted if I am completely honest, but in the mind of a thirteen year old, boys are usually somewhere on the list. In my case, I had it bad. A part of me thought he would make me wait a few days before calling, but I guess the curiosity was killing him too. While I was doing my homework and listening to music, the phone rang. No Caller I.D., no cellphones, no tablets, just me and the telephone. I let it ring a few times of course to disguise the fact that it was technically sitting on my lap. Well, here we go, the beginning of the rest of my life I thought, (*bringing the drama as only a true drama queen can*), "Hello", I calmly uttered waiting for a response. The voice on the other end asked, "Hello, may I speak to

Tamara?" It was Cool Dude and from this point forward we were inseparable, (*on the phone at least*).

Cool Dude and I talked on the phone for hours everyday but at school, not so much. He kept inquiring about why I would always act shy around him and the honest to goodness truth is I had no answer. We had great thirteen-year old conversation, he was handsome, and maybe even a bit cool and by all accounts, we liked each other the same, confirmation of this I received from Messy Girl who made it a point to tell me Cool Dude was always talking about me in class. Maybe I had judged Messy Girl unfairly, she seemed genuinely happy to share this information with me so I guess I will have to change her name, we'll see. At this point, things were going great, (*so I thought*). Talking for hours on the phone then ignoring him at school, the perfect combination for me, however, Cool Dude had other ideas and wanted my time and attention in public. At school, he began to make it known that he was unhappy with our current situation, he wanted more. More? More what? I had to ask. He wanted me to walk with him, holding hands, kissing, hugging, and cuddling, among other things I thought were reserved for adults. Is this boy serious? He can't be, but I soon found out how serious he was. He offered to walk me home the same day because he wanted a kiss. Completely taken off-guard, I wondered out loud, a kiss? What kind of kiss? Not a dry, unassuming peck on the cheek or lips but a slimy, sloppy, tongue-laced, spit exchange. The thought of myself willingly sucking saliva out of another human being's mouth made my stomach hurt and there was no way I would get over it before we got to my house. What was I going to do? He was expecting a kiss and I kind of, sort of agreed but there was no way in HELL it was going to happen. I knew this, but poor unsuspecting Cool Dude had no clue.

He walked me all the way home and I could tell he was excited to finally reach this moment. He was chewing gum, kept applying Chap Stick, grinning a little more than usual, in other words, he was ready. Dang, I thought, the closer we moved to the front door, how am I going to get out of this? I nervously looked for the house keys in my backpack, heart pounding, knees shaking, eyes wondering, in other words, nowhere near ready. My nervousness evident, Cool Dude grabbed my hand and pulled me closer to him, "What's wrong?" he asked, "Are you nervous?" I wanted to snatch my hand back and run away but that would have been weird, even more weird than this moment and I could not afford that kind of publicity at this point. If I could only hop on the nearest train back to Oakland, everything would be fine but that was not my reality. Reality was standing before me waiting to explore my mouth with his nasty tongue and although I hated to disappoint him, I did the unthinkable, the unimaginable, I told him I could not do it. His Cool Dude persona completely morphed into desperation. Why? What's wrong? Haven't you kissed someone before? Once again, I had no answers I just did not want to do it, so I didn't. Although he was obviously disappointed, he didn't get aggressive, call me names, or run off in disgust, he calmly took the loss and made a cool departure promising to call me later. I felt horrible, not because I refused to tongue kiss him but because I led him to believe I would. I kept replaying the scenario in my mind over and over again, thinking of how I could have handled it differently but no other scenario made any sense. This is who I was and I was not willing to compromise. Why did he have to go and mess everything up for a kiss? Boys.

Although I felt bad for what happened that afternoon, I was proud of myself for not giving in. I wavered between embarrassment to feeling empowered and then a little anxious to see how Cool Dude would respond to rejection. Surprisingly, he called me an hour or two after going home, we discussed the incident, laughed a bit and moved on. He promised to walk me home again the next day and by all accounts had already forgotten about our tongue kiss debacle. He is a Cool Dude I considered, until he walked me home the next day and it happened again, he asked me to do the tongue tango. Come on guy, what is your deal? I cringed. Can you just let it go already? A part of me wanted to tell him how annoyed I was that he kept asking for a kiss and break up with him, but I really liked him and wanted to keep him around a little longer, (*he was good for my self-esteem*). I tried to stall and keep talking but he wrapped his arms around my waist and went for it. "Wait!", I pushed his face back from mine. "We have to go inside because my neighbors will tell my Mom." Little did I realize they were telling on me anyway simply because a boy was walking me home everyday. I slowly opened the door and he quickly shut it behind me. I led him to my room, he grabbed my waist again and this time I didn't pull back. I wrapped my arms around his neck and began to kiss him but with no tongue, only small thirteen year old sexy pecks. He was clearly annoyed and you know what, I didn't care this was all I had to offer. Letting someone put their tongue in my mouth was not on my list of things to do. He left my house disappointed again this time suggesting

I was a tease and somewhat boring, buzz words that were obviously meant to draw a reaction of cooperation from me however, it did not work. Cool Dude kept calling me although he stopped walking me home, his conversations a little more aggressive than before.

Summer break was in a few weeks and I was going back to Oakland so that is all I cared about. He wanted to "hook up" with me while we were on break so learning of my plans to go back home for most of the summer, didn't sit well him. To make a long story short, I left for a month after school let out and returned just in time to find out my so-called boyfriend was having more fun with one of my acquaintances who had no issues doing the tongue tango and more. Suffice it to say, my shy disposition actually saved me from future heartache with this dude. Since all I had given up were my version of short sexy pecks, I had no emotional attachment to him so finding out about his new "love interest", meant little to nothing. I confess, I took a small shot to my ego but the experience was well worth it. I discovered I ultimately have the power and I would never allow anyone to make me do anything with my body I am not ready to do. I was made for great things, not sure what just yet, but the tongue tango at thirteen was not it.

6 THE MESSAGE

The key element in this passage is even though I was giddy about the attention I received from Cool Dude, it did not lead me to compromise my beliefs to keep him. No one should be willing to suppress the core of who they are to meet demands they are not ready to fulfill, especially young teenaged girls without a clue. Thinking back on growing up without a father, my mindset could have been worse. I could have acquiesced to Cool Dude and opened the floodgates to participating in other activities I had no business engaging in, all to experience affection from a male, something I was obviously missing.

Standing my ground in spite of the fact it meant I would eventually lose his admiration, meant everything to building mental strength and further highlights the necessity to set standards of accepted behavior and not deviate from them. This way of thinking directly defies what statistics say about young girls like me who grow up fatherless. If you believe the statistics, we are all gravitating towards every male who shows us attention because we long to fill the void left by our fathers.

While I understand this dynamic exists, one fact does not necessarily have to lead to the other. This is where role models in the family and community have an opportunity to play a significant role in changing the narrative, thus beating the odds. I have a long list of role models, some played a small role, while others turned out to be more significant than I realized. The point here is this: life hands us all a different set of circumstances and our ability or inability to successfully manage the good and the bad aspects, will depend on behaviors modeled before us, guidance from guardians, and our own determination to succeed. I had every excuse at my disposal to blame my actions with Cool Dude on growing up fatherless, and it never crossed my mind, because in the end, I wanted to be proud of myself. I needed to understand as early as possible that I control my destiny and to never allow someone else to do it. This was a crucial point in my growth as a teenager experiencing the highs and lows of life, and no doubt laid the foundation for future interactions.

7 CIRCLE OF FRIENDS

Summertime in Sacramento was brutal. I didn't want to come back to this place but I was needed to watch my little brother since my mom couldn't trust the neighbors to do so. Once again, I spent long, boring, hot, summer days in my new neighborhood. I met a few friends who lived close by so this helped pass the time, but I still spent my time scheming on how I could get back to Oakland. Since music has always been a love of mine, I would sit in my room for hours listening to the radio, writing lyrics to my favorite songs and recording myself singing them. I even started writing poetry. I created a book full of music and one for poems. I had vocals for a thirteen year-old, (*at least I thought so*), if only I could share this gift with others.

One afternoon, as I sat listening to music, the phone rang and Messy Girl was on the other end. I had forgotten we exchanged numbers and I was curious to know why she was calling. I immediately thought she was calling to be messy and talk about that dude, however, she did the exact opposite. She actually wanted to know about me, how I was doing, what I was doing, if I wanted to hang out, if she could come over and it was this very moment I realized I was wrong about her, she could very well be friend material. Even after this revelation I was still guarded because that is what Oakland taught me (*skepticism*) but I was more open to giving her a chance. My birthday was in three days and I was anxious to turn fourteen. This would mean a new beginning, high school, and even though I had new surroundings, I was both excited and curious. Excited because it meant I had reached the pinnacle of my school years, curious because the neighborhood bus that carried students to high school reminded me of Oakland. As bus number 10 passed by me everyday on my walk to school, boys were yelling out the windows, girls were talking loud, putting on make-up, it looked as if they were having the time of their lives and that is just what I needed. If only school started tomorrow, unfortunately, I had more than a month to wait. I wanted to go back home for my birthday but my mom still needed me so I decided to make the best of it.

Once again it was a million degrees outside but staying in the house just made me think of all the reasons why I hated this place. Still, I got dressed and headed out for what would later be deemed an adventure. I had two options, go hang out with the neighbor across the street who was younger than me and full of tall tales, or go further down the street to the neighbor who seemed a bit odd and out of sorts. Both of them were funny in their own right but I had to be in the mood to deal with them at the same time. Before I could make a decision, I see them both walking towards me in the distance. I started to turn around but didn't want to be rude, a decision I would later regret. Not because I didn't like the neighbor girls, (*they were alright*), but there was a dog waiting for us to reach its gate and when we did, it chased us more than a block back down the street. I was terrified of dogs so I yelled as much as I ran and when we reached my house, we laughed and laughed. The laughter soon turned to disgust when I realized I urinated all over my pants. Goodness! Was it that serious? Okay, I was officially irritated, it was hot as hell, there's a dog chasing me, and I peed my pants, (*playtime was over*). The Neighbor Girls thought my accident was hilarious and I could not get mad at them, I would have laughed at me too but nonetheless, I was still irritated. (*I knew I should have stayed in the house*).

For the next few days I did just that until my birthday July 15th, 1988, the BIG 1-4! We didn't do anything special, and besides, I was a low-key birthday celebrator who just wanted to get back to Oakland. It was Friday and my mom worked in Berkeley, her commute home was sometimes more than two hours, therefore anything we wanted to do had to wait anyway. Passing the time in my room with poetry and music made everything seem small. Music was my sanity and poetry was my remedy, we were so in love. Music in the form of rhythm and blues, hip-hop, gospel, pop, it mattered not, as long as I could feel it. There I was again basking in the glow of beats, rhymes, and melodies when the doorbell rang. It was Messy Girl turned good, wishing me a happy birthday, she called earlier asking if I was home so she could stop by for a few minutes, for some reason I wasn't expecting her to show up but I have to admit, I was a bit touched by her memory of my birthday and welcomed the company. She rode her beach cruiser all the way to my house in the sweltering heat.

Once inside, she handed me a tiny replica of a gift bag and inside was a pair of earrings, Salt-N-Pepa look-a-likes in silver. I was speechless and could not help but flash a huge smile and give her a hug. I had never received anything like this from someone I barely knew nor did I expect to, but nonetheless I thought it was special. This was the day I realized the value of true friendship. A person who thinks enough of you to take the time out of their day to make yours better, a gesture I would never forget. As she was leaving, my mom pulled into the driveway, said a quick hello and goodbye, and inquired about the identity of my visitor. I gave her just enough background to make a connection and my mom offered words of wisdom, "now that is a friend you want to keep around." I took her advice and for what was left of summer break we kept in touch.

8 THE MESSAGE

Friends are hard to come by especially when you're the new girl on the block. I just happened to meet the girls who would grow up to be my friends for life but I didn't know it yet. The person I labeled as messy turned out to be the exact opposite and the neighbor girls, although a tad bit different, were actually fun to be around. I needed to be more open to allowing space for new friends and although I was hesitant I began to soften to the idea. My mother's words of wisdom regarding the friend I unfairly called Messy Girl, resonated with me, as well as her kind gesture and I was willing to admit I was wrong. I cannot stress enough how my mother's guidance gave me the discipline I needed, but encouraged me to make some of my own decisions to prepare me for real life. In doing so, she gave me confidence in my own voice and a belief in myself that I am capable.

Sometimes I went a bit too far as a child interacting with adults because I was so used to being allowed to think and speak for myself, but in relation to handling issues with my peers, I was a step ahead of the game. My mom used to always remind me that the wisdom she shared with me came from my grandfather and great-grandmother and she thought it was one of the best gifts she could give me. Still, I was too young to fully process the magnitude of her words but I did however begin to internalize them. She would say things to me such as, "don't worry about things you cannot control", "be careful who you call your friend", "the world does not revolve around you", (*I think I heard that one a million times*), as well as, "speak your mind, but do so respectfully." I had no idea the effect these words would have on me but let's just say I have passed them down to my children hoping they will have the same effect. I truly believe my mental strength, balance, and independence derives from my mother allowing me the freedom to speak my mind and leading me to make decisions. When it came to friendships, she gave me her opinions and let me do the rest. Sometimes parents can be so overbearing and protective of their children that growth is stunted rendering them ill-prepared to thrive in the real world. Being allowed to take ownership in certain areas of my life carried over into everything I set out to achieve because not only did I want to make my mother proud but myself as well. Doing so meant I had to set goals and achieve them, be accountable for my actions, and stop acting like a baby because I moved to a new city, with the understanding that life goes on. Although I missed being back home, I began to do just that.

9 THE GUARDED HEART

Back in Oakland we were members of Bethel Missionary Baptist Church on 77th and E. 14th where we went almost every Sunday. I sang in the youth choir, my mom sang in the adult choir and by all accounts we were right where we needed to be. My mom became concerned that she had not found a church home for us in Sacramento but this soon changed when one of her coworkers invited her to New Testament Baptist Church.

The church was nestled on a corner adjacent to open fields that reminded me of farmland, further cementing my disdain for Sacramento, (*but that's not the point*). I did not know what to expect once we got inside but the parking lot was filled to capacity forcing us to park in the field. (*What in the world?*) I thought to myself and said out loud, this is crazy but it was another scorching hot day and I could not wait to get inside. As we walked into the doors we were greeted warmly and ushered to wait for permission to enter the sanctuary. Once the doors of the church opened we were seated in a section called "The Overflow" because there were no seats in the pews. It felt as if all eyes were on me even though I know that not to be the case and I hurried to a seat. While seated I observed what appeared to be the youth choir seated in the stand, an elderly balding man as the pastor and a number of ministers flanked around him. Typical of the Baptist church but I was more interested in hearing the choir perform because music was everything to me. As a minister spoke, I scanned the faces in the choir stand anxious for when that would be. A few more minutes passed as the announcements were being read and I was getting restless. Every word the announcer spoke was like a garbled message to me, they didn't even go in one ear and out the other, I never received them. I only wanted to hear the choir sing. Finally, the wait was over.

The choir director stood before the group and commanded them to rise, with his hands of course. He pointed at a short haired, fair-skinned girl to come forward and lead a song. She stepped to the microphone, the choir began to sing and what came next can only be described in that moment as magical. Every note, every melody she sang was heavenly. I was entranced. I could feel my body swaying to the beat feeling overwhelmed with joy and excitement for what I was hearing and witnessing. When the song ended I felt a sense of peace and a change of heart about living in Sacramento. I wanted to experience this every week. It didn't matter who preached, who read the announcements, or who ushered me to my seat, as long as this choir was a part of my life. This is the very moment that prepared me for the molding that would take place within me changing my outlook for the better. I was motivated during the week and could not wait for Sunday so I could hear the choir sing. My mom decided we would join the church and I agreed. The youth choir was my favorite and the adult choir was just as good. I learned and leaned on every word. However, when I finally built up the nerve to join the youth choir, bliss quickly turned sour.

At first, I wavered on whether or not to join the choir and one day decided to just do it. I loved to sing so I was very excited to sing with this choir and meet new people. I walked into the sanctuary and was greeted warmly and told where to sit (*I was an alto by the way*). The Songbird who entranced me the first day we visited the church was there and her voice was just as melodic as it had been every other time I heard it. I was absolutely in awe of her gift, which is why what happened after rehearsal was so disappointing. While I was socializing with a few of the people I met during rehearsal, an unfamiliar face approached me to deliver a message from Songbird. The message went something like this, "Songbird wants to know if you have a problem with her because you keep staring and if you don't stop staring, you will have a problem." The Oakland in me immediately surfaced and I tried to suppress it as best I could. With the B-word right on the tip of my tongue, I sent Songbird a message in return. "Tell Songbird to address me herself, otherwise I didn't get the message." Where I'm from that was the ultimate punk move, sending someone else to deliver an insignificant threat.

Needless to say, we did not get off to a great or even good start and it made no difference to me. Since then every time she led a song I had to work hard to separate the melody from the man, it was difficult but I pulled it off without a hitch. Although I did not like the person, her gift was undeniable and I was not one to front. We coexisted ignoring one another with occasional rolling of the eyes. It was both ironic and a shame that someone I had grown to admire in such a short time span would choose to address me in a threatening manner without knowing a single thing about me. My first thoughts of her were just the opposite but I was forced to defend myself because of course that is what I do, intimidation was not allowed and I could battle with the best of them.

Although I would prefer to be cordial with most people I meet, some don't deserve it and clearly she was one of those people. Still, I enjoyed church any way. I will admit that although I internalized the words we sang and hid them in my heart, I looked forward to socializing most. I met a lot of new people, boys and girls, some cool, others not so much but that's life. What mattered most to me is experiencing the melodies of music and that was my source of solace and refuge in church and in my room at home. At the time, joining this church was just what I needed, however, things started to get a bit interesting.

One night after choir rehearsal, a young man approached me because he was clearly interested in becoming my significant other. Once again I was flattered, but hesitant because I knew if I let him in that meant he would eventually want something from me that I was still unwilling to give. We exchanged numbers anyway and began talking on the phone every day. I was surprised to find out he was a little younger than me and that was a problem, but I decided to give it a try. I know I had nerves turning my nose up at a twelve year old when I had just turned fourteen but that year and a half is centuries when it comes to maturity.

Although he was very intelligent, the immaturity came through right away during our conversations. He was always bragging about how many televisions were in his household, while my thoughts were that he did not purchase any of them, his parents did, so actually they belong to his parents (*I wanted to say that so bad but decided I would be nice*). I guess that was his way of making an impression on me, as if somehow I would become the lucky recipient of one of those wonderful televisions if I chose to stay connected (*whatever*). Televisions must have really impressed the girls he was used to talking to, (*but trust me on this one, I could not care less about them*). T.V. boy was young but he was aggressive and quickly made it known what his intentions were with me, he wanted to be my man. Again, I was not ready for that but I pondered it because he was such a nice guy with interesting conversation, (*outside of his T.V. obsession of course*). He kept pressuring me to make a decision and I was holding back because a part of me wanted to just be alone. I told you I brought the drama like no other but I am also proud that being thoughtful protected me from a lifetime of pain in some respects. I would take simple situations so deep and analyze the hell out of them and this was no different, so I needed time to think.

T.V. boy grew impatient but stayed connected until I finally agreed to be his girl. If I am honest, a part of me thought since he was younger I wouldn't have to deal with the touchy, feely, kissy side of being a girlfriend, boy was I wrong! No sooner than I said, "Yes, I'll be your girlfriend", he was all over me with every opportunity. To make matters worse, my mom and his parents were friends so whenever she went to visit, he expected me to come with her. I did want to see him but I knew that meant he would want something from me. I just wanted to talk and enjoy his company without ending up horizontal or engaged in the tongue tango.

As time moved on, both were getting more difficult to avoid. One night we went up to his room while my mom visited his mother and things did not go so well. He expressed how he was growing tired of begging me for affection and wondered how long he could wait to receive it. This was déjà vu for me and still I was not moved, could not do it. From this point on, things were different. I stopped going with my mom to his house to prevent placing myself in sticky situations. We continued talking on the phone and at church but nothing like what he wanted and yet so perfect for me. We still called one another boyfriend and girlfriend, so I thought, until I was rudely awakened from this idea in the most disrespectful of ways. It was another warm summer weekend as our church prepared for the upcoming youth retreat at Camp Alta. By all accounts it would be a great weekend experience, one we would remember forever, and that was the honest truth. Both T.V. Boy and myself were planning to attend the retreat and even talked about spending "quality" time together if given the opportunity. Deep down I knew this would not be allowed so I felt less pressure to be a "girlfriend" on this trip. The bus ride up to the campsite was awkward as expected with both of us seemingly distant from one another as if we had not just talked about our plans for the weekend. Most of the choir members in our age range were on the trip as well which meant we were in for a drama filled weekend.

In some circles, T.V. Boy was a hot commodity so the competition was stiff, however, I had zero interest in competing for anyone who had not yet earned a space in my life. Thinking back, this was not the average train of thought for someone my age but I always knew I was special in spite of the fact that up to this point, no father figure was present to assure me of this. Yes, I was a little shy, awkward, and unsure of myself at times but if something didn't feel right to me, I was okay with letting it go. We completed the retreat activities for the day, ate dinner and were given free time to roam the campsite. T.V. Boy went his way and I went mine. Free time comprised of hiking, campfires, storytelling, and socializing. When free time was over, we were instructed by the camp leaders to come together for a final meeting. One leader led a group of kids down a hill and I looked up just in time to witness T.V. Boy walking hand in hand with a girl from the choir who obviously tickled his fancy in more ways than I cared to engage. I would never have walked hand in hand with him especially in this setting, so for all intents and purposes, he made the right decision. I stared at him the entire walk down the hill as he struggled not to gain eye contact and in this moment the only emotion I recall feeling was relief.

I spent the rest of the retreat ignoring both him and her, as I anxiously waited for the moment it would be over. I was then, and remain today, a "never let them see you sweat" kind of girl, (*unless it is my husband of course*). He can make me feel and display a variety of emotions without even trying but that's not the point I am making here. T.V. Boy made his decision based on what I would not do with him. He detailed his feelings in a letter he later gave me explaining how he regretted this decision and wanted me back. At this point I had already moved on, not to another relationship but it didn't matter, I was unwilling to reconsider. If this was the type of boyfriend he would be, I would not be signing up for the sequel, furthermore, he had a chance and as the saying goes, you never get a second chance to make a first impression. I was no longer interested or available. Once again, I felt empowered because I had no doubt, protected myself from future heartache. If you did not earn me, you definitely do not deserve me.

10 THE MESSAGE

During this time, Sacramento was beginning to feel more and more like home and New Testament Baptist Church had everything to do with it. Sure I was disappointed that Songbird delivered a "mean girl" message to me but if that was the worst thing to happen, so be it. I attribute my resiliency and mental strength to my upbringing and previous experience with being let down. It wasn't the first time and likely would not be the last and I was okay with that. It is a good thing my mother prepared me for moments like this because I otherwise may have crumbled under the disappointment of being treated so rudely by someone I had grown to admire since visiting the church. I was proud of the way I handled her idle threat and even felt more empowered that she was clearly thinking enough about me to send a message. The encounter had the exact opposite effect on me than what I am sure she intended. In my opinion, I had Songbird right where she deserved to be, in the back of my mind. I was too busy being caught up in the music, building my character, and learning about my spiritual connection to God. Every word we sang as a choir I hid deep in my heart making it difficult for anyone or anything to send me to an unhappy place. Not even T.V. Boy with his antics. Oddly enough, my situation with Cool Dude prepared me for what T.V. Boy did. It's amazing how life presents us with trials to make us stronger and we never know why these things happen until we are forced to face them again. While neither scenario was a big deal, that is precisely the point.

Young, impressionable teenagers go through scenarios like mine every day and even though I was able to handle potential heartbreak with my head held high, not everyone takes rejection lightly. I also believe that not having a father in my life taught me to deal with rejection, something that my mother helped me navigate through her consistent displays of positivity. Although I never mentioned either incident to my mother, her influence over the outcome was prevalent. I would rather take a small hit to my ego than allow myself to be controlled by the desires of someone else. In these instances, I had officially learned the value in loving myself thus preserving my integrity and character. A lesson I would carry with me from this point forward.

Please understand these were clearly learned behaviors modeled before me and we do our children a disservice when we coddle them instead of empowering them. The ability to see myself as the victor and not the victim in these scenarios was a direct result of empowerment, encouragement, and confidence building from the person who knew me best, my mommy.

11 SCHOOL DAZE AND SOUL MATES

My freshman year of High School had finally begun and I could not have been more excited to begin this chapter in my life. The complete chapter would be a few more months away since we found out our freshman class would be bussed to a local Junior High School due to asbestos at Hiram Johnson. It was a bummer but I made the best of it. Regardless, I chose to look at it as being in high school.

I made so many new acquaintances over a small span of time and it only enhanced my outlook on what was to come at the main high school. If the rest of my high school years were anything remotely close to the first few months, I was in for the time of my life. Happiness is the best way to describe my feelings. I loved my classes, the teachers were cool, the boys were cute, and most of all, I was finally settling in. Even though on most days I still preferred Oakland, I was finally beginning to consider Sacramento my permanent home and actually becoming okay with it. I had classes with what I call some of the funniest people I had ever met, some of the smartest, some of the coolest, some of the quietest, even more quiet than myself, (*now that was a revelation*). I just remember loving everything about it, the Class of 1992 was everything, Little Rapper Boy included. I am almost certain there had to be a few bad days my ninth grade year, however, I am unable to recall them. It was literally bliss and only got better and better once we were cleared to go to the main campus.

Our first day at the real high school was everything I had dreamed. The entire freshmen class was split up into groups and assigned Senior Buddies. The high school powers that be had smiled on my group and sent us two of the most beautiful Senior Buddies a freshman girl could ask for and the mile wide smiles we displayed said it all. The Senior Buddies showed us around the school, gave us a few tips about high school survival and in essence welcomed us to the real world. Well, as real as it could possibly be for freshmen boys and girls and we enjoyed every minute of it. I recall one of the Senior Buddies commenting on our cheesy grins, insinuating that we could tone it down a bit, at the time, that comment flew right over our heads.

In my eyes, high school became a fast-paced world of fun, laughter and excitement that I had never envisioned. The dances, the boys, the football games, the basketball games, the social clubs, all in one location, and I tried to do it all. My freshman year was definitely one to remember.

Although I had major interest in boys, I still had little interest in having physical contact with them, talking on the phone and at school was it for me. I was never a touchy feely person to begin with and the older I grew, I could see the potential for problems. Thankfully none that were earth shattering but enough where people began to take notice. I had lots of friends who had friends, and their friends had friends so I often found myself in situations that had little to do with my friends of choice. Some of the experiences were awkward and others just plain weird mostly due to my observations of them and their observations of me that I am sure were not favorable as mine often were not favorable of them either. While I was never one to be moved by popular crowds, I always managed to be in the mix of them due to the friendships I forged. I remember some of the juniors and seniors would ask me, or one of my friends about why I seemed so shy and quiet and my response was to smile and say, "I am just observing." This really was the honest to goodness truth. I have never been one to fraternize with people I didn't know in order to appear sociable or cool. Through my observations, I would determine who I felt was worthy of my time and attention. Once again, I know this sounds a bit nervy of me but I was very protective about who I socialized with and popularity meant nothing. My new high school friends would laugh at me because they noticed it too and likely weren't quite sure what to think of it either but nonetheless, they allowed me to be me.

Speaking of new friends, they included the person I once named Messy Girl, now she is Smiley, for obvious reasons. I had completely misjudged her and now considered her a friend. Another of my friends included one of the Neighbor Girls, only because the other was two years younger than us and not in high school yet. There were a few others I had only become acquainted with in the first semester but wasn't quite prepared to call them friends. Life at the main campus was a totally different world from our time at that local middle school. The campus was huge and even though most of the freshman classes were in portables, you could easily get lost in the shuffle. Smiley and me had a couple of classes together but our Math class was the highlight of my day.

We had a sarcastic, dry-humored, smart-mouthed teacher named, Mr. Lawless (*to protect the innocent*). He and Smiley would periodically get into classic, borderline disrespectful debates about his teaching style and her constant chatter, and whether or not a combination of the two contributed to her lack of understanding the math concepts (*If you asked me, it was his style*). He was all

over the place trying to teach concepts I am still not sure
he fully understood himself.

As I recall, only a few people in the class understood
his style of teaching, one of them was an acquaintance
who refused to help us when we asked her questions
because I am sure she enjoyed feeling like she had the
upper hand. (*Whatever she needed to do to help her self-
esteem, go for it*).

In spite of the fact that math class was difficult,
Smiley and I enjoyed our time immensely. I especially
enjoyed the boys. There were so many to look at and of
course that is all I wanted to do. There was one in
particular who caught my eye. He was fair-skinned, with
a low haircut, and beautiful hazel, grey, or green eyes
(*whatever the color, they were dreamy*). I never had the
nerve to ask him which color but either of those I viewed
as gorgeous and so was he, (*at least in my mind*). I was
running my mouth a little too much in gym class about
my infatuation for Dreamy Eyes and word somehow got
back to him. I only knew this information because his
friend confronted me about it and tried convincing me to
just talk to him (*well we all know that would never
happen*). He even gave me Dreamy Eyes' number
encouraging me to call him (*why was he so concerned
over whether or not I called someone else?*). Either he
was just as shy as me or something fishy was going on, I
thought. While I was not quite sure what was up with
Dreamy Eyes, something didn't sit well with me, so our
relationship was strictly "Hi" and "Goodbye." He would
walk by me in the hallway flashing his signature smile as
if he knew something I didn't, but things never went any
further than that, (*good*). Once again, I was conflicted
because although I wanted to get to know Dreamy Eyes

better, I was never going to press the issue because in my mind, boys weren't interested in what I was interested in, *(all I wanted to do was talk)*.

Still, it did not matter what they wanted but how I felt about giving it away. "It" did not necessarily mean sex but any piece of my time, heart, love, and affection was mine to give and I was openly selfish about when, where, how, and who to give it to, simple as that. If I'm being completely honest, it also had a lot to do with the fact that exchanging spit and other bodily fluids grossed me out so, needless to say, I was fine with getting a simple smile from Dreamy Eyes. Another example of how I sought to preserve my mental and physical well being through thoughtful consideration of situations I allowed myself to entertain. The interesting fact here is back then, I didn't fully understand the gravity of my choices.

As freshman year progressed towards the end, my thoughts turned to spending another hot summer in Sacramento. This time around, however, I was looking forward to creating my own sunshine no matter what it took and thankfully I did just that.

Summer break in our neighborhood started out uneventful until we had a few visitors to "the circle." That is what we called the cul-de-sac where we lived that was nestled in the middle of a long block seemingly in the middle of nowhere. It was a quiet unassuming neighborhood other than the sounds of children playing and laughing the days away. A world of difference from the hustle and bustle I became accustomed to growing up and in some respects, it was just what I needed. Maybe this was precisely what my mother had in mind when she made the executive decision to move us away from home.

Whatever the reason, I had finally warmed up to this place just in time to meet my Summer Crush.

I saw him a few times before at church but never talked to him because he appeared to be quite the ladies man. Girls would flock around him I'm guessing because he had a nice smile, boyish charm, and he seemed to be friendly with everyone, still, I was not yet impressed. I remember finding out from one of the girls in the choir that although he had a few admirers, he already had a girlfriend, someone I knew of but not acquainted with at all, and apparently he was also interested in someone in the choir. Why I was told this information I am not sure, (*maybe I had a look on my face that said I wanted to know*). The entire scenario sounded annoying to me and wasn't anything I was interested in involving myself with, which made it even more surprising when he one day showed up at "the circle."

All of the kids in our circle and neighboring block would gather around talking, listening to music, playing tetherball, bike riding, you name it, we did it. It was a known fact that summer nights in our neighborhood were comic relief because something was bound to happen. Kids would fall, fight, get chased by dogs, play the dozens, fall out one day and become friends the next, typical child's play, which made things even more interesting when a visitor showed up, a boy, to be specific. I will call him Mr. Smooth. As it turns out, he was visiting one of my childhood friends across the street to attend his upcoming birthday party, and this friend just so happened to be his cousin. At first, I tried acting as if I didn't notice him. I had a sly way of appearing not to pay attention, when I really was and I have to admit, I was really paying attention. In addition to having a gorgeous smile full of white teeth, he was funny and actually fit right in to "the circle" since by all accounts everyone thought he was pretty cool. He added to the excitement of those hot summer nights giving me something to look forward to everyday, but I would never tell him that. I began to notice he was taking an interest in me because I would catch him staring and he would constantly find any reason to speak to me. Although I was secretly flattered, I heard him tell someone he was only visiting for a week and leaving after the party, which meant he had one day left and not to mention, a girlfriend, so he was off-limits in my mind. Another day passed, which meant our visitor would be leaving soon and honestly I was a little bummed about it. I wasn't quite ready to say I liked him, but I was definitely intrigued.

Later in the evening after the sun went down, I was getting ready for the party when there was a knock at the door. I quickly opened it thinking it was one of my friends but it was Mr. Smooth himself inquiring about whether or not I was going to the party. I started smiling inside and tried not to on the outside (*since I stayed in guard your heart mode*), but let it go anyway. My smile forced him to do the same. "Why do you ask?", I responded. He wanted to make sure I was at the party since this was his last night in "the circle." I say sarcastically, "Don't you have a girlfriend?" To my surprise, he said, "not anymore" (*When did this happen? I wondered*). I was already going to the party but now I had extra incentive. "Yes, I'm going but I am waiting for my friends then we will head over", I said, trying to play it cool (*I know he did not think I was going to show up to the party with him*). He smiled his approval and headed back across the street.

When my friends showed up, I wanted to mention the visitor I just had, but decided I would keep it to myself so they wouldn't get the wrong idea. After the fiascos I have had at the ripe age of fourteen, (*clearly drama*), I was not going to assume anything. We made it to the party, which was held in the garage. The lights were dim with music playing, people and food all around and I could barely walk two feet before Mr. Smooth grabbed my hand asking me to dance and I quickly turned him down. I was not the dance with boys at a party kind of girl, even though I wanted to be this time. He kept asking me over and over making it difficult to keep denying him, (*but kept denying him*). He was the exact opposite of my shy introverted self and that's what I liked about him. He made me laugh when I didn't want to, made me smile when I was trying to be cool and had me thinking about him when we were apart (*who is this boy and where did he come from?*).

For the first time in my young life, I felt a real connection to the opposite sex but instead of embracing it, I was terrified. Terrified because this time was different. While I liked or was infatuated with others before, I never felt this vulnerable and for that reason, I was hesitant to allow myself to let go, especially since I had recent learning experiences with so-called teenaged love. It feels like we were together all night talking about everything: his now ex-girlfriend, why they broke up, how he always liked me but thought I was mean, how he thought about me all the time, and even got the okay from his cousin on choosing me (*Huh? First I think you need to make sure I want to be chosen, sounded good though*).

The rest of the actual party was a blur, but Mr. Smooth and I, clearly enjoying each other's company, were disappointed it had come to an end. He asked if I wanted him to walk me home but since I came with my friends, I was going to leave with them as well. Although I wanted to leave him with a hug and a kiss (*surprisingly*), a smile and a sweet goodbye worked perfect for me. I was on cloud nine when I got home and before I could put on my pajamas and get ready for bed, the phone rang. It was Mr. Smooth (*of course*), and we spent the rest of the night on the phone, laughing and talking, getting to know each other very well. I dreaded the next day because it meant he would be going home leaving me to anxiously await the moment we would see each other again.

The next day Mr. Smooth called me early in the afternoon to tell me he would be staying with his cousin for two more weeks. I was excited yet a bit apprehensive because I knew the longer we enjoyed each other's presence, the moment would come that expectations of me would not be fulfilled. My time spent with Mr. Smooth seemed nothing less than magical (*well at least from a fourteen year old point of view*), yet I knew the ride would undoubtedly end once he discovered my anti-intimacy rules for dating. For the time being, I simply enjoyed our interactions for two extra weeks.

Surprisingly, he never made an advance indicating he wanted something from me. There was just good conversation (*borderline silly at times*), laughter, and more fun at "the circle." Two weeks quickly passed and this time Mr. Smooth went home. By this time, I had grown comfortable enough with him to share a bit more of myself than usual so the content of our conversations escalated into more personal topics.

One day while talking on the phone, Mr. Smooth asked me about my dad, I don't recall the exact response I gave him but I was flattered by his growing interest. He seemed to be genuine in his presentation, which only intrigued me more. However, on a sadder note, he was preparing to leave again. This time he was going back to his hometown of Flint, Michigan for a visit with his mother for the remainder of the summer. He moved from Flint to Sacramento to live with his dad and he went back to Flint every summer. He told me he would likely not be able to call me long distance but would definitely try, to which I silently grinned my approval, hoping his efforts would pay off. Before we hung up the phone he said he had an important question for me. I could tell he was nervous so it must be something serious (*I thought*). It seems as if it took him ten minutes to get it out but once he did, it was music to my ears. He asked if I would still be his girl when he came back to California (*Although I didn't realize I was his girl, I was ecstatic he had already claimed me*), I agreed and from that point forward we were history in the making.

Needless to say, the summer of 1989 was special for me and at the young age of fifteen, it defined the strength and character that would ultimately carry me through life symbolically unscathed.

12 THE MESSAGE

Starting high school can be difficult, especially in a new environment, but for me it was the turning point where I began to realize I ultimately had control over my thoughts and actions. This meant that no matter what anyone else thought of me, the perception I held of myself would determine the path I take. In some respects I could be vulnerable, sensitive, and a bit awkward, but I was also stubborn, determined, thoughtful, passionate, strong-willed and self-aware. The combination of these characteristics sustained me in the face of criticism, peer-pressure, rejection, and in my new surroundings. As I began to adjust, the wall I built was slowly deconstructing. However, this wall I am referencing had been a symbol of protection for me, preserving my integrity while saving me from the pitfalls of teenaged love, and for that I am grateful.

On the other hand, the wall was also a crutch, one that I would use to shut down and separate myself from discomfort thus making me avoid situations where the outcome may not have been favorable. Even though, in my mind, I was being protected, I made further attempts to block myself from experiencing hurt when in actuality, hurt prepares us for real life. I am in no way suggesting I should have allowed myself to be hurt in my relationships or anyone else for that matter, I am simply acknowledging the flip side to building a wall of protection as a means of getting through life. I knew all too well the hurt and disappointment that comes from growing up without a father but that was no excuse to allow others to do the same. In this respect, the wall worked for me and in many ways was necessary.

I honestly believe the way I maneuvered through life was a direct result of the uncertainty I felt about being a fatherless child and in order not to appear vulnerable, I was deliberately the exact opposite. Once I met Mr. Smooth, I was conflicted by his genuine nature and my skepticism. I am the type of person who believes people have to earn their place in your life and as a teenager that concept was not lost on me. It was not enough to be charming, persuasive, handsome, funny, and intelligent, I needed consistency above anything else. People will usually show you who they are within a small timeframe if you are patient and observant, and although I was drawn in, self-preservation was still the goal. One might wonder if it was fair to require consistency from teenagers who were in search of themselves as I certainly was, but that line of thinking misses the point that it wasn't about them, it was about me. I was the one who needed to establish standards of how I would allow myself to be treated. I could not afford to leave my well being to the discretion (*or lack there of*) of horny teenaged boys on the prowl for conquests. Setting standards demonstrates self-love and self-awareness and also holds others accountable to respect said standards or risk being blocked out. I made no exceptions and if Mr. Smooth could not handle this he would not be allowed in my world. I know to some this may seem a bit presumptuous, however, just know that loving and caring for ourselves sometimes requires us to be unwilling to compromise, even when we are infatuated. I was definitely infatuated with Mr. Smooth but I never compromised who I was to be with him. In fact, he would compliment me on my love-me-or-leave-me mentality and how I never tried to be anything or anyone other than myself. He thought my mental strength was attractive and made him even more intrigued. The fact that he recognized this and was okay with it, told me that he would be a keeper.

For the next few years, (*outside of a couple of break-ups here and there*), we were inseparable. Although Mr. Smooth admired my efforts to be self-assured, oftentimes it became more than he wanted to deal with so the break-ups were necessary. Admittedly, I could be more than a handful at times but once again, all of my actions were intended to preserve myself and protect my heart, so while I am not proud of some of my melodramatic behaviors, they did just that. I had no idea how long Mr. Smooth and I would last, but one thing I was sure of is we shared a special bond, which made our break-up in the summer of 1996 shocking (*to me at least*).

13 THE CATERPILLAR

It had been at least a year since Mr. Smooth and I broke up and during this time frame, I immersed myself into church activities, mainly singing in the choir and Wednesday night bible study. Not because I was down trodden, but it was more a time of reasserting my spiritual walk. I never stopped going to church while I was with Mr. Smooth, but a lot of my time was consumed with our relationship. Even though I missed him, I was content with being alone so I didn't rush into another relationship. I used this time to figure out what I wanted from life and how I was going to go about getting it. Was I going to stay in school? Start working full-time? What would my life look like in five years? All the possibilities a goal-oriented twenty-three year old should consider.

My friends were also my strength during this time. Whenever we were together, it was nothing short of fun-times and happy days, with every outing proving to be more adventurous than the next. I don't know what I would do without my friends. Through good and bad times we have stuck together, even when we got on each other's nerves. I don't believe they realize how much of an impact our friendship had on me during this time, and this is why we are sisters for life. My friends would rarely ask me about my and Mr. Smooth's break-up and rightfully so, it wasn't that big of a deal in the grand scheme of things. I went out on dates with a few nice guys, unfortunately, the majority of them were not ideal for me. I dated a college football player, a momma's boy, a stalker, a narcissist, a free spirit, a pretty boy, in other words, every facet of the personality rainbow, so no one can say I didn't give it a chance. I just wanted more out of life and therefore required more than any of them could offer at the time, (*to be frank*).

It was actually a good thing I had the opportunity to date a variety of personalities because I had been with Mr. Smooth for so many years, I needed to experience life outside of our relationship. He spoiled me to the idea that everyone would be as patient, understanding, and loyal as he was and I needed to see, first hand, that this was not the case. I am sure he felt the same because when you are with one person for so long from an early age, you begin to wonder if you are missing out on a better relationship. I initially believed Mr. Smooth was my soulmate but once we broke up, I acknowledged how wrong I was.

A second year passed since our break-up and I had grown comfortable with the idea that we would never get back together again. My thoughts were confirmed when I found out he had a girlfriend. Although I was okay with us not getting back together, I have to admit my stomach turned a bit at the thought of him being in another relationship and it was made worse by the phone call I received one day out of the blue. Mr. Smooth and his new girlfriend had apparently gotten into an argument and he called me venting about it (*I immediately went into ex-girlfriend mode and wanted to hang up on him, but I didn't*), surprisingly, I listened. I wasn't sure if he wanted my advice or just wanted to tell me his side of the story, furthermore, I wasn't even sure if I should be offended that he had the nerve to call me about his girlfriend in the first place. Why did he feel comfortable enough to tell me about their argument? Why was I listening? It was a strange scenario if you asked me and I wanted out of it, but for some reason, I stayed on the phone, even offering my advice on how he should handle the situation (*that was big of me, I know*). One piece of advice I offered, (*albeit half-heartedly*), was for him to stop telling her, "my ex-girlfriend would have NEVER done that", not a particularly good way to end an argument *(this made me smile and told me in his own way, he still cared)*. He agreed and after I let him get out all of his frustrations, I calmly reminded him how so very simple his options are: "either you are going to deal with it or not, but whatever you decide, make sure you are ready and willing to live with it" (*a piece of priceless information I received as a child*).

After we hung up, for a minute I felt like I had been sideswiped onto the side of the road, however, after careful thought, it occurred to me that it was actually very mature of him to call and share his relationship troubles (*and might I add, even more mature of me to listen*). This very moment proved we had more of a bond than even I realized, he actually thought of himself as my true friend. Although we were no longer together, there was still an obvious connection that even a new girlfriend could not replace. I was flattered by this fact yet I didn't take the implications lightly. I just kept a level head, keeping in mind that I truly believed we would never get back together.

Coming up on our third year apart I began to date a guy I met at the mall a few months before. Although he was handsome, that was pretty much it. I honestly cannot recall what convinced me to give him my number (*I was usually very particular about who I gave my number*). The conversation was bland, he couldn't articulate his goals for the future, and he was too dependent on his mother, so by the third or fourth date, I decided enough was enough. I let him down easy but firm in order to prevent a misunderstanding and he reluctantly moved on. I say reluctantly only because he had twenty questions about how I had come to my conclusion and wondered how he could fix things. He even added that he had just come out of a long-term relationship where he was deeply hurt by his ex-girlfriend and may have been a little distracted. I assured him we would not work well together and moving on would be the best scenario for both of us, just as I had done to the dates before him (*well one guy I just ducked and dodged because he wouldn't take no for an answer*). I couldn't understand why I ended up meeting so many guys who were completely wrong for me. It truly baffled my mind to the point where I decided to take a break from it all. No more giving my number out, no more chance meetings, and no more dating (*Until I figured things out, it will be just me, myself, and I*).

As soon as I made this declaration, days later, Mr. Smooth called again, this time to invite me to his twenty-fifth birthday party. There was no mention of a girlfriend in this conversation and I didn't know what to think so I calmly inquired about date, time, and location, adding that I would try to make it (*knowing full well I intended to be there*). The party was more than a week away, which made the next few days seem long as I struggled to settle my curiosity about Mr. Smooth and his girlfriend. At first, I was just going to show up without knowing but as the day drew near decided I'd better ask. If I am perfectly honest, I was not interested in going to his party to watch him with his girlfriend. I ended up calling and found out he no longer had a girlfriend. I didn't ask the usual when, where, why, and how, I just needed to know, especially since I played second fiddle to no one. Mr. Smooth of course, wanted to know why I inquired (*as if to insinuate this meant I was expecting something*), but that information I politely kept to myself (*he didn't need to know any more than that anyway*).

The day of the party had finally arrived. Choosing not to attend alone, I called my friend Smiley and she agreed to accompany me. There were several guests present when we arrived and even more showed up afterwards. Mr. Smooth greeted us at the door and we were escorted to our reserved seats. It was a bit awkward seeing him after so much time had passed but we both smiled uncontrollably at the site of one another. I didn't want to read too much into what this meant (*self-preservation at its finest*) but I did get that butterfly in the stomach feeling I had when we connected for the first time at a party as teenagers. The irony of so many years passing between that moment and this one was nostalgic, taking me back to the beginning of where it all started.

Mr. Smooth kept checking on me at our table as he worked the room greeting all of his guests. How we ended up in this space ten years later can only be explained as a spiritual connection that was meant to be. As the party came to an end, Smiley and I decided to leave and Mr. Smooth walked us out the door. He commented on how nice I looked and that he was glad I showed up. He also let me know he would call when he got home because we had a lot of catching up to do. In that moment, I accepted it and would no longer fight the feeling. I was also glad I went and once again, from this moment forward, we were inseparable, this time, forever.

14 THE MESSAGE

During the three years Mr. Smooth and I were apart, instead of focusing on rebounding with the next man, I took the time to self-reflect, spend time alone with myself, and ultimately, achieve a closer spiritual connection to God. Often, we become distracted by things that are of no value to our growth as human beings, thus stunting our growth in relationships; with mates, friends, relatives, co-workers, and even strangers. As I stated before, my mother raised me to treat everyone the way I wanted to be treated, keeping this in mind, I believe I deserve the best.

People often asked me how I went three years without having a significant relationship after being with Mr. Smooth for so long. The simple response is, I love myself therefore I am okay not being in a relationship. I had a great time learning more about who I was as I met different individuals, being able to decipher between wants and needs. During that time, I didn't need a boyfriend, I needed to know that a relationship did not define me and was not the most important aspect of life. Sure we all want someone to share life and love with but when you share them as someone who is truly not whole, the relationship often lacks substance.

Coming to the realization that as an individual I am in control of my happiness was liberating and once again allowed me to see myself as the victor and not the victim. Even through the wall I erected to protect myself, I learned that there were times I could be vulnerable and it was okay. There were certain people I didn't have to be guarded with and could still protect my heart. The way I chose to deal with relationships and the possibility of them was to always think of myself first. I know this is selfish but at the time it is what worked for me since I didn't have a male presence in my life to direct me in this manner. I had to figure things out on my own so if I erred on the side of caution to protect my well being, (*then selfish is what I had to be*). I usually looked at the bigger picture and what it would mean for me to continue interacting with someone. I also recognized how they spoke to me (*tone, respect*), the topics of conversation (*content*), the friends they associated with, and reputation, either through questioning or a familiarity with their history.

As I type the characteristics I looked for in relationships, it appears more involved than it actually was as it usually takes little to no time to figure out where someone stands if we pay attention. For example, one of the men who attempted to date me, made his attempt through a coworker we had in common by asking him to give me a message. At first, I was a bit annoyed by the fact he had not approached me himself but decided to give him the benefit of doubt since he worked predominantly in the field. I gave the coworker my number to pass along to him and he called me the same day. During our brief conversation, we asked the usual questions, (*Do you have kids? What are your likes and dislikes? What are your goals? Where do you see yourself in the future?*), by all accounts, the conversation was going pretty well until this happened. The guy asks me, "How old do you think I am?" Not realizing this question would be a set-up for the end of the beginning, I replied, "I would say 30 or somewhere close to that", upon which time I received an emphatic, disrespectful (*in my opinion*) response that went, "FOOL! I am not 30, I am 25 years old!" My immediate response was to proclaim the conversation as being "Over!" I no longer wanted to chat with the man I had already given the benefit of doubt in the first place, he had no more chances with me, I was done.

Needless to say, we never spoke again and he regarded my unwillingness to carry on as unreasonable and snobbish. Once again, it mattered not what he thought of me but how I viewed myself. If I allowed him to get away with calling me a fool during our first conversation, he may grow comfortable enough to call me other disrespectful names and I was not willing to stick around to see which ones. To be clear, I never thought I was "better" than him or anyone else, I simply felt I deserved the best, which does not line up with allowing myself to be mistreated or disrespected in any form or fashion, simple and plain. When you truly love yourself the way I had grown to over the course of years, establishing standards of expected behaviors becomes the norm rather than the exception. This is why Mr. Smooth had so much leverage with me because even though he could be sarcastic and smart-mouthed at times (*myself as well*), he was caring, kind, considerate of my feelings, patient with my stubbornness, consistent, and most of all, loyal (*this means a lot to me*). As I list a few of his positive attributes, it made me think of why we even broke up in the first place, and that is just the point, I cannot recall. Mostly due to the fact it obviously wasn't an earth-shattering event, but I choose to look at it as a break-up that was mandatory otherwise we may not have remained together today.

For a majority of our teenaged years, and into our early twenties, we were all each other knew and I believe we were both in need of experiencing life away from one another. Understanding this dynamic played a huge role in why I was content when we were apart. I didn't need a relationship to define me instead I had to learn to define myself in order to figure out how a relationship would fit into that equation. I am not saying I knew we would get back together because I honestly thought the opposite, but it was more a sense of believing that no matter the outcome, I would be just fine (*self-preservation in full effect as usual*). This is how I make it through life today, even when a circumstance knocks me down momentarily, I know I control whether or not I stay down or get back up.

15 BREAKING DOWN THE WALL

Not long after the party, Mr. Smooth and I got back together and on Valentines Day the following year, became engaged. It was a wonderful time in my life and I felt it was only right that he and I were together. The interesting aspect of us getting back together is had he not reached out to me, I likely would have never reached out to him for a reconciliation. I say this because I had long moved on in my mind (*so I thought, or rather convinced myself*), and out of fear of being rejected, I would have stayed away. That is the good and the not so good about self-preservation. I was always concerned with protecting myself that I ran the risk of losing people who meant a lot to me, because I meant more. Like I said before, this is a risk I was willing to take since self-preservation worked for me. Thankfully, in the case of Mr. Smooth and I, it worked to perfection.

Exactly fourteen months to the date we became engaged, we were married, April 14, 2001. Almost ten months from the date we were married, we welcomed a beautiful baby girl, February 11, 2002. Our lives had been forever changed. The years following the birth of our daughter were difficult as we struggled to merge thought processes, ideas, beliefs, and expectations under one roof. I had my way of thinking and believing and he no doubt had his, but there was one thing neither of us could dispute, the adoration he showed for our daughter. From the moment she was born, he took ownership and never let it go. He would feed her, change her, bathe her, dress her, take her to daycare and wake up in the middle of the night with her. She would fall asleep on his chest after he rocked her for hours, and wake up in the same position. One day the daycare provider asked me,

"Which one of you is rocking her to sleep every day because she will not take a nap unless one of us rocks her, so please stop it!" To which I politely replied, "Talk to her Daddy", but it didn't do any good, no one could tell him what to do with his daughter. She was the apple of his eye, and rightfully so. (*To this day, nothing has changed*). Watching the relationship they have, brought up feelings in me about being a fatherless child that I never knew existed (*or at least I blocked out*). I often wonder if I did not have a daughter, would I have ever realized or acknowledged what I missed. While I don't have a cliché story about waiting on my father to pick me up after promising he would, or sending me gifts that never came in the mail, I just never expected anything from him due to there was no precedent set that either would happen in the first place. I used to always say, my mother was both a mother and a father to me and therefore I did not miss out on anything. In hindsight, that was just another way of protecting myself from being hurt by his absence, something I had mastered because no matter what, life goes on.

As a child, I only remember one time where I was obviously disappointed about my absent father but moved past it quickly because I didn't want to appear ungrateful for what my mother had already done. I have no clue where this mindset came from at such a young age, but the only thing that makes sense is that it is all related to my purpose in life. I was meant to go through certain things in order to gain the perspective I needed to be an example for others who may have difficulty in this area of life. Although I was strong and independent, watching my husband and daughter interact daily, forced me to acknowledge that in spite of the fact I was raised well, I indeed missed out on a bond that a mother's love can never replace. I did have periodic contact with my father here and there but he was never a consistent presence, not enough to make a positive impact. In spite of this, I turned out to be a capable, intelligent, level headed (*most of the time anyway*), caring human being who desires to reach my full potential, and see others do the same. I like to think of my story as a part of the process to getting where I am today, but for my experiences, I may not have the same mindset.

When I think back on my experiences and the many times I had an option to do the wrong thing, it never felt right. That is in no way a suggestion that I always did the right thing but in most cases, I did, or at least tried my best. I may have learned after the fact that I made the right decision but I never allowed the opinions of others to drown out my own. I am a person who thinks and feels my way through situations, sometimes to a fault, but the point is I think for myself. I am aware of the research that correlates fatherless children to bad decision-making, lack of direction, juvenile delinquency, poor achievement, criminal activity, teenaged pregnancy, substance abuse and much more. Keeping this in mind, one could surmise I had every reason to take the wrong route but I always knew there was something special I needed to share with the world, it just took some time for me to figure it all out.

When I was younger I thought it was singing and poetry. Writing poetry and singing in my room for hours taught me self-expression and about my ability to string together words into whatever form I chose for whatever I wanted to say. In many ways, music and poetry also taught me to feel, to be intuitive, to self-reflect, how words can express our innermost thoughts, and most of all, the power I possessed. I only discovered my writing ability through listening to music and internalizing what I heard. Music was my sanity while poetry helped me express emotions that were often held back. I could be whoever I wanted to be and feel the way I wanted to feel at any given moment. I was free to exhibit self-acceptance even if others did not accept me. My world of poetry and song was powerful and I am convinced they are a huge reason I was able to cope with situations that may have otherwise succeeded in leading me down the wrong path.

Another reason for my strong sense of self-love came from unexpected yet appreciated sources because it really does takes a village. First, there was my uncle back in Oakland who would always call me Little Whitney. He thought I looked so much like her growing up and to me that was the ultimate compliment because she was my idol. To know that I could be compared to someone I held in such high esteem made me smile inside and out even though I couldn't see the resemblance. In my mind, she was the ultimate beauty and I didn't compare, but as he kept saying it, I started to believe it and that had a huge impact on my self-esteem. At this stage in life, I had a long way to go but my uncle was the first man to tell me I was beautiful and it meant the world to me. It is amazing how something as small as this can have so much meaning but when you put it in proper context, it was necessary.

Another positive male influence on my self-esteem was from one of the leaders at the church I grew up in once we moved to Sacramento. He was like a father to me. From the first day I met him, he was so enthusiastic and always made it a point to tell me how "gorgeous" I was. He was also very encouraging, and genuinely interested in seeing me succeed in life. At first, I wasn't able to receive his compliments without feeling uncomfortable and that was the problem, I had it all wrong, they were not compliments but affirmations of who I already was, which worked to build an even greater sense of love for myself. I am not sure he even recognized the impact his words had on my self-esteem (*I recently told him in person how much his encouraging words meant to me*), but I am grateful he saw something special in me during a time when I was still finding my way. While I understand I am not defined by beauty, and that is the premise we need to teach our children, feeling good about myself in this respect led to higher levels of acceptance regarding other attributes I had yet to discover. How many of us know women who are extraordinarily beautiful yet still lack self-esteem and self-love because no one encouraged and loved them? Positive words have the power to influence children to greatness, just as negative words have the power to lead them astray. I shared these examples to demonstrate the positive impact of a few adults in my life who took the time to pour greatness into me through encouragement.

Even though I had a wonderful mother and upbringing, there was no male presence, so my uncle and the Church Leader filled in the gaps. Another aspect of my life I never gave any thought until I was old enough to assess the impact. I don't want to give the impression that if I never received these affirmations, I would have jumped into the arms of the first male who complimented me, but I am thankful I will never know. In saying this, I turn my thoughts to the young girls and women who never had a father or anyone show them love, care, or concern, the many young girls who yearned for their daddy's presence and as a result, were never quite comfortable in their own skin. Remember, these young insecure girls become insecure women who are often unable to cope, unable to love, unable to be loved, unable to effectively communicate, and thus unable to live. I am one of those fatherless girls who persevered in spite of, and it is my intention to empower other little girls, pass the insecurity and doubts created by such a circumstance. I need to demonstrate that it doesn't have to define the rest of your life, but let it be inspiration to succeed.

Growing up without a father is not the worst thing that can happen to anyone, especially when the mother can somehow compensate for the loss, but to act as if there are no residual effects (*as I did growing up*), is disingenuous and dangerous. It is better to deal with the issue rather than ignore it in order to be completely honest about your feelings so they can be purged instead of carried through life from relationship to relationship. I had the opportunity to purge feelings about my father and once I did, I was free to help others through the same circumstance.

Today, I have a relationship with my father, obviously not one representative of the bond that's formed in childhood, but it works for me. I don't expect any more from him than he gives because I am satisfied that my purpose in life is being fulfilled through his absence. I recognize this is a mature and wise place to reside, in light of the circumstances, but it takes more energy to be negative and pessimistic. Energy I do not wish to give.

16 THE MESSAGE

While I never chose to acknowledge it as a child, the impact my father's absence made on me was undeniable, manifesting itself through the relationship I witnessed between my husband and daughter. Watching their interactions stirred up feelings in me I never knew existed, forcing me to open old wounds, something I fought hard to ignore. When I look back on the way I dealt with this circumstance, it was clearly a method of self-preservation, as I only wanted to acknowledge the positive aspects of my childhood. Focusing on the negative meant I was somehow identifying as a victim, someone I never wanted to be. Besides, I was in control of my happiness and would not allow the actions of someone else to be the standard by which I determined how happy I should or could ultimately be. Still, it was important for me to acknowledge my feelings even if it took thirty years to do so. Keeping these feelings locked up created blind spots for me where I made decisions in life out of fear of being hurt without actually assigning the credit to my circumstance. I am still not sure if I should give growing up a fatherless child credit for being overprotective of my feelings because it gives the impression that this was a good thing. It did however make me more cautious about whom I allowed in my space and for this I am grateful. I am also grateful that when I was finally forced to deal with these feelings, it was within the confines of a loving relationship and after years of building a strong foundation of self-acceptance, which made it easier to cope, the key item here being self-acceptance.

Accepting everything about my existence, flaws and all, was the catalyst for dealing with life and its many pitfalls. I believe this is one of the major elements missing from parenting today. In many ways, children learn behaviors that teach them to be the victim instead of the victor, which creates a woe is me mentality and feelings of inferiority. These feelings often cause children to lash out irrationally, or become withdrawn to the point of depression due to a lack of direction or credible role models in the home. I understand there are exceptions to every rule and some parents are truly giving their all to ensure their children grow up to be productive citizens in society. However, the fact remains, too many children are hurting and falling through the cracks as their feelings go unrecognized and unharnessed for a lack of understanding of the depths of their internal pain and conflict. Often, this pain can be alleviated through consistent encouragement, (*as in my case*), reminding children they are worthy, they are loved, they are powerful, they are talented, and can achieve any goal they set out to accomplish.

My story is indicative of a young girl who could have chosen to play the victim and allow my circumstances to dictate my future, but the consistent encouragement I received, never gave me an opportunity to be self-defeating. Although I created defense mechanisms, as I grew older, the encouragement I received in my formative years, made a world of difference to my self-esteem. For this reason, I am inspired to do the same for others, starting with my own children. Since they were old enough to talk, I have been busy encouraging them, planting seeds of positivity in their minds, hearts, and spirits, so they understand their own power and how not to give it away. I constantly remind them to treat people the way they wish to be treated and to carry their selves in a manner that represents self-love. I share my experiences with them as an example of overcoming negative circumstances and to demonstrate that I too was once a child with some of the same issues they have and can therefore relate.

My husband is also a beacon of positivity so they get a double dose of it regularly and it is evident in their strong but friendly personalities. I am now beginning to see the effects of our encouragement manifest itself in the way they believe in their abilities to be whatever it is they desire in life, an accomplishment that as a parent, makes me proud. I in no way want to coddle them into a state of victimization, doing further harm than possibly any outsider has the power to accomplish. I embrace my responsibilities as a parent, understanding the positive and lasting impact my mother had on me and attempting to recreate the same or similar impact on my children. My mother's influence, among other contributing factors, created a strong-willed, self-loving, self-accepting, competent, level-headed, powerful woman and I would be remiss in my duties as a mother, if I kept these gifts for myself. Furthermore, I would be remiss in my duties as a human being, if I chose not to share the gifts I received with the world. I wholeheartedly believe that God blesses us so we can in turn bless others so who am I to sit on any of my blessings as if I somehow was not the beneficiary of someone else's. I am aware I cannot save the world but I can definitely share my experiences and in doing so if I have a positive impact on the people in and around my life, or even those I come in contact with, mission accomplished.

As an adult, I have had countless opportunities to positively influence the lives of others, and it never gets old. It is a natural way of existing where often times, I gain insight as well as different perspectives, which allow me to remain open-minded in my approach. Keeping this in mind, I am aware we all have different ways of existing, which means my way of dealing with personal pain and conflict may not work for everyone, but one point we should all agree on is personal issues with internal pain and conflict should be addressed. If my journey has taught me anything, it is that unacknowledged pain doesn't go away, but continues to build symbolic mountains in our path that eventually we must climb. It is my purpose to help as many people as I can possibly reach with climbing those internal mountains that refuse to go away with time.

17 DEALING WITH CHANGE
Journal Your Thoughts

Dealing with drastic changes in life such as moving from one city to another, can be difficult but do not have to be if you can learn to put the changes in proper perspective. As a teenager, moving away from everything and everyone I knew was difficult for me to grasp, so I spent a great deal of time fighting it by leaving Sacramento every chance I could get. However, what I didn't realize initially were the positive aspects of the move.

During this time of transition, I found solace in writing poetry and journaling. I wrote poems about many different aspects of my life, people, and surrounding environment. I would write about the positive and negative aspects of moving to Sacramento without knowing the effect it had on my perspective. Although there were a number of circumstances that added to me growing comfortable in a new city, journaling my thoughts allowed me to clarify my feelings until I reached a point where it wasn't as bad as I initially thought. Sometimes it takes seeing your thoughts on paper before gaining proper perspective and ultimately realizing things could be worse. Journaling did just that for me, it helped me see the silver lining in the clouds I created. Sure, change can be difficult, but there are always opportunities to make the best of it, you just have to be open-minded and willing to adjust. I like to believe that everything happens for a reason, so instead of focusing on change as a negative, find your purpose in that space of change.

Understand Change Can Be Good for You

Change can occur in an instant, or gradually over time, and how well we adjust to change depends on an ability or inability to adapt. Adapting to change helps us to discover abilities we may not have realized had circumstances remained the same. Change also teaches us to be flexible in our thinking, at times, our own rigidity can be stifling, and damaging to personal growth, keeping us stagnant and set in ways that are no longer of value. While it is not necessary to discard every aspect of who we are to deal with change, we must be willing to evolve as individuals, especially in situations where we have the opportunity to positively impact the lives of others. Change can also strengthen us in areas of discomfort or unfamiliarity. Stepping outside of the comfort zone, as I have, is both rewarding and life-changing.

Living through change has empowered me to accomplish many things, which I likely would have never attempted had change not been prevalent. You might not be reading this book today if change was not constant in my life. I worked for a company for more than twenty-years and in November of 2014, the opportunity for change presented itself and I took a leap of faith and left the company. I always understood my purpose was greater than my wildest imagination, and it took me to become accepting of change, even in discomfort, to find and fulfill that purpose.

Choose a Positive Attitude About Change

When all else fails, a little positivity goes a long way. Positive attitudes about change and life in general, is a choice. Choosing to be negative strips us of an opportunity to see the bigger picture and ways we can be impactful in spite of our discomfort. Yes, at first I hated everything about moving to Sacramento until I started to recognize that my attitude needed adjusting. No matter how negative I remained, my mother was not moving back to Oakland, which forced me to live with the decision. Sure, I could have continued on in a negative place but that would have proved detrimental to my overall psyche` possibly affecting areas of my life that mattered most, such as self-esteem, education, family and friends.

If you think about the many people we come in contact with daily, especially those in our household, we can positively influence others in ways we have yet to uncover. I understand some people view positive habits and lifestyles as a fairytale, and negativity as being a realist, but what's the harm in being both real and positive about our circumstances. I could not imagine living an existence where everything I considered to be real is negative. With this way of thinking, there is no room for hope and faith, only a defeatist, victim, crab in a barrel mentality that keeps reminding you of your shortcomings yet ignores your ability to overcome.

Optimism is the faith that leads to achievement; nothing can be done without hope.
- Helen Keller

18 COMFORT IN YOUR OWN SKIN
Stop comparing yourself to others

Many of us fall under this category in one way or another, depending on which areas of life negatively affect us the most. Some of us have a low body image, lack confidence, wish we were prettier, smarter, more athletic, etc. No matter what your struggle may be, it becomes reality to you when you constantly remind yourself of **perceived** shortcomings. Comparing yourself and perceived shortcomings to those in and around your life, does little for your self-image, yet creates more insecurities about living up to ideals set by someone else. Besides, things are not always what they appear to be in the lives of others. Instead of focusing on comparisons, use the skill, intelligence, hard work, and determination one uses to achieve goals as motivation for you to do the same. Furthermore, comparisons are often obscured by a false sense of identifying with people and things that have no value in the grand scheme of things. In these instances, little significance is given to one's own personal abilities and accomplishments, which should undoubtedly be the focus. To achieve a positive self-image, look no further than yourself for solutions.

Define Yourself

As adolescents, we reach a point in life where we are "trying to find ourselves", in search of the happy medium between "fitting in" and forming our own identity. Along the way, there are moments, and unfortunately people who seek to define us in ways that do not align with our own thoughts and ideas. Perception being reality is the driving force here because people tend to form opinions of others either: a) based on what they have heard, and b) based on a small sample of interactions and observations. For these reasons, perceptions can be difficult to change, however, this should not be your concern.

Defining yourself and not allowing others to define you is of the utmost importance and essential to developing a positive self-image. Examples of ways to define yourself:

1. Journal thoughts about how you view yourself

2. Celebrate YOU, flaws and all

3. Analyze your inner circle of family and friends

4. Speak and act in ways that parallel your goals

5. Be consistent

Journaling thoughts about how you truly view yourself, encourages you to not only reflect on the positive aspects of your existence, but also helps you identify the negative traits in order to use them as a reference for personal growth.

Once you uncover your true self, celebrate those traits, even the negative, because they have worked to form you into the individual you are today. Acknowledging that you are not perfect helps you to forgive yourself for your shortcomings, paving the way for a more positive self-image. Your inner circle should consist of people who both challenge and encourage you to be the best you can possibly be, whether through words or deeds. Many times our inner circle includes individuals who don't have our best interest at heart and instead of encouraging you to be great, are secretly wishing for you to fail. Be wise and humble in your selections! Many people speak about themselves in terms that do not match their actions. For example, if you believe you are capable, professional, goal-oriented, and worthy, carry yourself in that manner. Being consistent is the best way to reinforce the best parts of you. Make a daily effort to be great at whatever it is you do.

Be ALONE With Yourself

One of the best ways to get to know yourself is to spend quality time ALONE! We get so used to having people in and around our lives that we forget to spend time enjoying ourselves. Time alone can consist of taking walks, long drives, having talks with ourselves (*out loud even*), journaling our thoughts or whatever activity that can be done ALONE while fostering a healthy self-image. So many of us are afraid to be alone for a number of reasons. Some of the most common reasons being, the need for validation, comfort, companionship, and even for the sake of appearance. Please understand that when you truly value yourself, you don't need others to validate you, they only enhance or confirm what you already believe. I am a writer so you will often hear me suggest journaling as an escape or remedy for whatever ails you. Growing up, I kept a journal that eventually led to discovering my gift in writing. I began to write poetry, which led to writing songs and most recently books. The point is, journaling allowed me to discover great things about myself at a young age, that I otherwise may not have known. Don't be afraid or ashamed of the person you are, just be great at being YOU. Before this can be accomplished, you have to know who YOU really are.

Our experiences, environment, and circumstances play a huge role in how we think, act, and live. By the same philosophy, the way we view ourselves plays a huge role in the company we keep, the way we treat others, and the way we allow ourselves to be treated. Make the time to cultivate and nurture the best parts of yourself so that you can recognize your own value, which in turn forces others to see it as well.

Remove Negativity from Your Life

Too much of what we see on television, (*some reality shows*), social media, in our lives, and the lives of others is negative. The more negative energy that surrounds you, the easier it is to adopt a negative disposition. For those of us who are already prone to negativity, it continues to feed the need for drama and conflict. The simple solution is to rid your lives of all things negative that clearly are stunting your growth into more positive ways of thinking and existing. Refuse to watch the show that stirs up the need for conflict and confrontation in you. Refuse to listen to the song that provokes your spirit to wrath and reject the negative banter from the mouth of your friends and family. In other words, make room for more positivity in your life. The more you surround yourself with negativity it becomes difficult to relate to a more positive way of thinking. For example, the negativity you see will become normal prompting you to dismiss positivity as somehow being a fantasy that is not within your reach. Think about it, if your thoughts, conversations, disposition, and entertainment are all of a negative nature, where is there room for a healthy self-image? The answer lies in your ability to refocus and begin to relate to more positive aspects of your existence. Again, journal positive traits and characteristics about you and use them for positive reinforcement, refer to them daily. Read them aloud until you believe it. This exercise forces you to speak life into yourself, making it easier to speak life into others, thus providing a foundation for the healthy self-image you should have.

Shine Your Light

Once you are well on your way to having a healthy and positive self-image, make every effort to shine in all that you do. Whether you work for yourself or someone else, present the best YOU and watch everything else fall into place. Shine your light wherever you go; at the grocery store, at the local gym, at a department store, at the post office, at church. I guess you get the picture, leave a little shine wherever you set your feet. I understand there will be days when you don't feel like shining but you don't have to wear that fact on your face and in how you dress. Taking care of the outer you is also important to achieving a positive self-image. Instead of wearing sweats and a T-shirt to the store, one day, throw on a nice casual outfit accented with a smile. People are naturally drawn to those who make an effort to look presentable. What you will find as your self-image becomes more positive is your standards in how you present yourself will increase. The more you feel better about yourself, you will become aware of your surroundings and will be more deliberate in your choices. This includes friends, social gatherings, entertainment, etc. Shine your light like only you can, the point being, no one else is YOU. We are all unique individuals here for a purpose and when we focus on anything and anybody other than ourselves, we miss an opportunity to create our own shine built on the very purpose of our existence. No, you cannot make people love or even like you. No, everyone is not your friend. No, everyone is not going to support your vision. Yes, people will let you down when you need them most, and you know what? SHINE on anyhow!!

*Most of all, never forget that there is no brighter light
than the one within you.*
- Jacqueline Schiff

19 FULFILLING YOUR PURPOSE
Identify Your Gifts

In my opinion, unfulfilled purpose is one of life's greatest tragedies that can be avoided if we are honest in our self-assessments and in tune with our natural God-given abilities. Not everything you love to do should be classified as a gift or your purpose. Some people are naturally talented in several areas of life but gifts are representative of a passion and purpose brought forth to positively enrich or impact the lives of others. Everyone is born for a purpose, and it is up to us as individuals, to discover our purpose, and work daily to fulfill it. My purpose was revealed to me after many years of interacting with family, friends, coworkers, and strangers. Through these interactions I began to make the connection between the reactions I received for giving advice, displaying a positive attitude, sharing encouraging words, a genuine smile, and having a heart for what is right. Identifying the connection influenced me to use my gift for the good of helping others recognize their own power. Our gifts are meant to do just that, impact the lives of others in a way that encourages belief in one's own abilities to succeed and live a purposeful life. Use your gifts wisely, as they have the capacity to be both powerful and life changing.

There is nothing quite as potent as a focused life, one lived on purpose.
- Rick Warren; Pastor, Author

Acknowledge the Power of Your Gift

Many years after recognizing the gifts I possessed, which were intended to fulfill a purpose, I was stuck between fear and doubt. Fear, because although I understood my gift, I was more concerned about how it would be perceived by others. Doubt, because I put limitations on my ability to make a real impact in the lives of others. Both of which stunted my growth, momentarily causing me to become complacent in a dead-end career and the completion of educational goals. I had completely downplayed the power of my gifts until one day it finally struck me, this is not the way I should be living my life.

From this moment on, I began the process of completing my Bachelor's Degree in Communications and researching diverse career opportunities. It wasn't so much that my career and education were exclusively tied to my gifts, but seeking to accomplish great things in those areas of my life and ultimately achieving them, instilled confidence in me to accomplish anything. My gifts never changed but were enhanced by my newfound mentality of self-efficacy through achievement, which forced me to acknowledge the power of my purpose and how to walk in it.

After all preparations have been made, all excuses laid aside, then you must not be afraid to act.
- Bishop T.D. Jakes

20 DEALING WITH HURT
Acknowledge and express feelings

Masking true feelings about being hurt is not the best way to address the scars created by the circumstance. I learned how true this statement is when I was forced to acknowledge the pain of being a fatherless child. As I mentioned before, during my childhood, I don't recall ever feeling one way or the other about his absence, but as I learned later in life, there were clearly hurt feelings. My choice to never acknowledge the hurt was rooted in a belief that I am a victor and not a victim and although this is true, unresolved issues remained. The better choice for dealing with pain would have been to open up to someone about my feelings in order to create an opportunity for healing.

Although it took me more than thirty years to reach this point, once I shared my feelings, the healing began. I was then able to reach out to my father without feelings of resentment because I placed his absence and my subsequent feelings in the context of it fulfilling my purpose. I don't hate him, nor do I speak ill against him, I forgave him, as I understood that this was a part of my journey, right or wrong, and no amount of anger and resentment can change it. Forgiving him was necessary in order for us to have a relationship, and in spite of the pain he caused, I grew up to be a pretty decent human being.

Forgive and truly move on

When you find it in your heart to truly forgive someone who is the source of your pain, it demonstrates maturity and an ability to step outside of your feelings to see the bigger picture. Although I eventually forgave my Dad, there was a point where I began to resent his perceived slights at my importance. I had it all figured out in my mind that he was the one missing out on a wonderful daughter and how it was a shame a father could ignore such a unique, loving, and intelligent human being and that someday he would regret it. However, this way of thinking kept me in bondage to my pain, demonstrating I had not truly forgiven him and moved on. It was as if I wanted to now hold on to the pain I fought many years denying existed. How quickly the tide changed once I could actually see and feel the hurt but at this point, it was my responsibility to get over it, not his. Sure, he is my father and in many respects owed me his presence, however, as an adult I could not afford to be bound by his inaction. I had to take control of my feelings, find it in my heart to forgive, and move on, and that is what I did.

Forgiveness is letting go of the pain and accepting what has happened because it will not change.
- **Judith Mammay**

21 DEALING WITH PEER PRESSURE
Be Yourself

The best way I have handled peer pressure in my lifetime is to unapologetically maintain a healthy sense of who I am, which acted as a buffer to any pressure I may have faced. I was not concerned with "fitting in", and "wanting everyone to like me", so my mentality was to think of my feelings first and not what others thought of me, I was genuinely okay being the odd man out. What I found is people respected me for my independence and in some ways wished they had the same. Being a "loner" in theory was a big deal for me because it meant I had complete autonomy over my actions without interference from my peers.

Even though I had many friends, there were times when I did my own thing. Not because they were awful people, simply because that is who I am. My friends would make fun of me from time to time, laughing at my adamant refusal to participate in certain activities but they understood me and often remarked, "That's just Tamara." Me being different didn't matter to them, and my friends never tried to make me feel bad about my differences (*not that it would have mattered anyway*), the fact that we were friends is what mattered most. There are several types of peer pressure and not just related to children and teenagers, adults can experience levels of peer pressure as well. Whether you are a child or an adult, the key is to recognize you ultimately have control over your actions and reactions and anyone who claims to be a "friend" should respect that and not try and force or shame you into doing something you are uncomfortable with, in other words, if this is an issue for you, find new friends.

Follow your inner light to your own personal greatness, and remember that you are admired and loved just as you are.

- Jacqueline Schiff

22 PREPARING FOR A RELATIONSHIP
Make Sure You are Prepared for Commitment

I have had discussions with men and women who proclaim they are ready to be in a steady or committed relationship, but for whatever reason, finding the "perfect" mate has proved difficult. One of the questions I often ask is, "Are you really prepared for a committed relationship?" The reason I ask is often times people want to be in a relationship for fear of being alone (*so they settle*) or because they genuinely believe they are ready until they discover the opposite (*they are not ready*). Relationships are a lot of work, especially when there is a commitment in which both parties involved need to be fully prepared to participate. When I say fully prepared, I am referencing having the presence of mind to understand completely what a committed relationship entails as well as determining your capacity to be what someone else may look for in a mate based on your own expectations. In other words, are you willing and ready to be everything for someone else that you will require of them? This is an important question to consider, especially since we tend to have these exaggerated lists of characteristics we want in our mates. Think about it, the average list of traits we look for in a mate include: 1) handsome/beautiful, 2) funny, 3) tall, 4) rich/independent, 5) nice figure, 6) pretty teeth, 7) intelligent, 8) patient, 9) family-oriented, 10) adventurous, to name a few.

Using this particular list as a reference, are you prepared to exemplify the same traits you expect from someone else (*since your dream guy/girl will no doubt have their own list*)? The point of this passage is to work on becoming the things you want your mate to be and maybe you will attract someone who fits the description. While it is unreasonable to expect perfection, we all can stand to improve ourselves in one way or another. Never get to a point where you stop working on bettering yourself. Whether in or out of a relationship, self-improvement is necessary, as it is how we grow as individuals. Growth allows us to gain new perspectives on what are the most important aspects of life and relationships. As you grow, in many respects, your lists will begin to reflect that growth, and it is up to you to prepare for this moment.

Do Not Settle

I once engaged in a conversation with a woman I had just met about whether or not settling in relationships was a good or bad idea. Let's just say the conversation quickly turned into a heated exchange (*however still respectful*). My position was obviously that one should never settle for mediocrity in order to be in a relationship and my counterpart's position was that she did not believe settling was a bad idea. The problem with this line of thinking is that you actually give yourself permission to accept less than you deserve or desire for the sake of being in a relationship. This goes back to my assertion that people often get in relationships for fear of being alone. It that's the case, call it what it truly is and don't try to disguise it by creating a rationale for settling.

Instead, deal with the root cause of why being alone is such a scary or negative prospect for you. In the long run, many people discover that settling is often more costly than being alone, (*as my counterpart later confessed*), and the residual effects can be heartbreaking. Save yourself the time and heartbreak by requiring more from others as a demonstration of genuine care and concern for yourself, and people who don't have good intentions for you will eventually be weeded out. Those who intend to do right by you will stay, and others simply will not.

23 ENCOURAGING CHILDREN
Don't Miss An Opportunity to Be Impactful

One of the reasons I was able to thrive as a child is the encouragement I received from certain adults in my life which helped me find balance in a world where I had little. The importance of role models and encouragement from adults is often understated but for me it was huge. It made a world of difference in how I viewed my abilities, future, my overall existence, and myself. I felt as if nothing was impossible for me to achieve and no one could stop me from achieving it (*but myself of course*). I was empowered to be the very best, on the shoulders of the people in my life who regularly poured positivity into my spirit. Understanding the impact it had on my life, influenced me to pour into children in the same manner. I make it a point to encourage children no matter who they are because one never truly knows the depths of pain for a child struggling to find their way. Yes, children are resilient (*as I am constantly reminded by child development experts*), but they are human beings who need nurturing, love, support and guidance to navigate a world that can be so cruel and unrelenting.

Take time out today to encourage a child, you could be the catalyst for building confidence and self-esteem which carries that child to greatness.

Drop a pebble in the water, and its ripples reach out far, and the sunbeams dancing on them, may reflect them to a star.
- Joseph Norris

Encourage a Victor and Not a Victim Mentality

Growing up, my mother empowered my brother and I by allowing us to speak our minds as long as we were respectful, which often created a fine line that I crossed many times. She would tell us that our opinions mattered, even when talking with adults, but we had to learn to demonstrate self-expression with boundaries. Most of us are familiar with the expression, "Children are to be seen and not heard", but this way of thinking does more harm than good to building self-confidence. I am unsure of where this expression originated and even more confused as to why it was later adopted into society, but children need to learn the value in self-expression as it demonstrates for them the power in their personal abilities and also that they matter. It teaches them to speak up for themselves and to not be intimidated by peers, something that is highly necessary in reference to the bullying that takes places in our schools and in life. Children need to be prepared to deal with peers who may try to intimidate or pressure them into situations they are uncomfortable engaging. In my opinion, to raise a child that is only seen and not heard, creates a social imbalance that they very well may not recover from thus rendering them a victim of circumstance.

Children are "little adults" that we are responsible for preparing to succeed at high levels in life and should therefore teach them at an early age that their voice matters, (*within reason of course*). I constantly encourage my children to speak their minds because I will not always be there to do it. I need to know that they can survive in this world without me, so my job is to prepare them for this occurrence. At the same time, I am an advocate for my children, demonstrating to them that as an adult, I will care for and protect them, but will not hesitate to admonish them when necessary. My children understand, as I have made it clear, they are ultimately responsible for their actions and in doing so, I must also prepare them for that responsibility. Children who are seen and not heard represent powerlessness, (*although some will argue its discipline and respect but that's a debate for another book*), which is in direct opposition to empowering them to deal with the cruel realities of this world. If children are left unprepared, they are in essence, victims, so we must teach them to be victors with limitless power and potential, and it begins with allowing them to have a voice.

24 SELF-EXPRESSION
The Power in Self-Expression

When it comes to being self-expressive, I never have a problem speaking my mind, since I was encouraged to do so as a child. This is a trait I carried into my adult years while encouraging others to do the same because of the liberation it brought me. Throughout my journey, I have found self-expression to be soothing for my soul. When I have something to say, and I am passionate about the subject, it sits on my chest until I can release it. I could not imagine living life not being able to express my feelings, either for fear of what others may say, or even worse, because I lacked the ability to do so.

Self-expression not only gave me a voice, but confidence in my thoughts and subsequent actions without seeking approval from others. For this reason, I encourage my own children and people I interact with to find their voice, be deliberate, and to boldly speak the truth, as they know it. We all have something to say and therefore should not be dismissed or discounted. Sure we won't always agree and will undoubtedly share perspectives that are based on our life experiences, but that is what makes us individuals. My story is not yours, and yours is not mine, but nonetheless, they are equally important. Finding the balance between my reality and being accepting of others are what contributes to my well-rounded disposition of learning from and welcoming different perspectives. A major reason for conflicts we experience in relationships, no matter the title, is a lack of respect for the other perspective. We are naturally selfish with our opinions but it shows a great deal of growth and maturity to recognize the value in someone else's perspective, even in disagreement.

Moreover, self-expression matters for everyone as it provides a glimpse of our innermost thoughts and fears, and is, once again, soothing for the soul.

Journaling Your Thoughts

At an early age I learned to write out my thoughts in a journal, diary, notebook, self-made binder, it didn't matter, I just wrote them down. Although I didn't realize it at the moment, journaling proved to be a powerful way for me to express my thoughts and feelings. This also helped in piecing my thoughts together when interacting with others because I had a frame of reference for topics that were of the utmost importance to me. How many times have you gotten into discussions, debates, arguments, or just passion driven conversations only to later discover you failed to mention a few important details that would have added more perspective to your position? How often have you said things you really didn't mean due to a lack of finding words that truly convey what you meant to say? Journaling can help you fix this. I know pen and paper is not popular in today's smartphone, laptop, social media driven society, but trust me journaling helps you to become more in tuned with your thoughts, thus giving you power to accept who you are as an individual. When I journal, I write about my likes, dislikes, wants, needs, desires of the heart, positive and negative attributes, goals, life experiences, and more. In other words, I learned to become comfortable with myself even as I recognized flaws. Journaling also highlighted my love for writing. I would think of creative ways to describe myself, and the people around me, using poetry and fictional stories, all of which acted as a barrier to negative influences that tried to overtake me. I often hear people suggest they are not very good at writing and would rather not journal, but keep in mind, these writings are only for you to see unless you choose to share, so formatting, grammar, spelling, and sentence structure are irrelevant. Never allow perceived deficiencies to deter you from becoming the best you can possibly be.

25 NEVER IGNORE RED FLAGS
Set Boundaries and Stick to Them

This topic is a favorite of mine because I believe every bad relationship had red flags in the beginning that were either ignored or accepted. Since I learned about red flags early on in life, and became quite familiar with them into adulthood, I was comfortable addressing them and moving on but I find that with some people I know, it is just not that simple. Please understand that your willingness to accept bad or indecent behavior is a direct result of how you feel about yourself and what you deserve from a relationship. The example I provided earlier regarding being called a "fool" during the first few minutes of a conversation, demonstrates my low tolerance for disrespect, as well as expectations on how I believe I should be treated. Granted, fool isn't the worst thing I have been called, but in the context of a relationship, especially in the beginning stages, it is completely unacceptable to me. I get that my standards may be a bit different than someone else's but the one thing we can all agree on, is there should definitely be boundaries set for behaviors that will not be allowed. It is often too late to wait until relationships grow to a more serious nature because then emotional attachments take place, making it more difficult to react rationally to unbecoming behaviors. Cut your losses before investing time and energy that can be used in more productive relationships.

I have had the opportunity to speak with women, single and married, about this topic and one thing each group of women have in common is acknowledging the red flags they saw but ignored for whatever reason. I know it seems cliché when discussing "red flags" but reality is many people are operating in unfulfilled relationships, or even worse, in relationships they have no business engaging in because they failed or refused to address them. What's wrong with holding people accountable for how they treat you? What's wrong with expecting to be treated with the utmost respect? Why is it okay to accept poor behavior from a mate? Why even consider it? If you find yourself constantly being treated in a manner you know is unacceptable, work on the part you ultimately control, yourself. Although you can't force people to treat you as you wish to be treated, you can make it plain to them by not accepting the behavior and moving on. Nothing says "I LOVE ME" more than setting boundaries and sticking to them.

Red Flags Are A Preview of What's To Come

In the beginning of most relationships, people are on their best behavior in an obvious attempt to get close or closer to the object of their affection. The problem is, when it's not real, it doesn't last very long because the true YOU eventually comes out and this is when the red flags tend to appear so pay close attention. Red flags can be subtle and overt (*like the "fool" debacle*), and can also be confusing causing you to question whether or not the behavior should be considered a red flag, just know that if you are confused, err on the side of caution. It is better to let it go early on than to figure out down the road, you've made a mistake.

I have been told that I am a bit hard on guys when it comes to relationships, but I believe differently, I don't think it is asking too much to expect my mate to be a genuinely good human being. Do you? Red flags are not always about how you are being treated, it can also include how this person treats others. Again, my standards may not be the same as yours, but I want to encourage you to look at the bigger picture (*instead of waiting for hindsight to be 20/20*), we can learn a lot about people by the way they treat others. One thing you can certainly count on is the fact that if in the early stages of dating you ignore red flags you will have to deal with similar behaviors in the future. People are who they are so don't fall into the trap of thinking you can change them, you cannot. Don't misunderstand me, I do believe it's possible for people to change, but change has to come from within and not because someone else wants you to do it, something I thankfully figured out early on.

Recognizing and then reacting to red flags I detected

was another method I used to preserve and protect myself because that is what was important to me. Ultimately, it will depend on what matters most to you as to whether or not red flags will make a difference, just keep in mind that you are doing yourself a disservice to simply ignore them.

RED FLAGS That Are Commonly Ignored

Aggressive language/behavior: One would think this red flag is self-explanatory, unfortunately, that is not always the case. One person's interpretation of aggression may not meet the standards of aggression for someone else. Since my tolerance level for it is quite low, being called a "fool" is verbally aggressive to me. Actually, any form of name calling not considered a term of endearment (*honey, dear, sweetie, babe, you know, the usual*) should be unacceptable. In addition to name-calling, aggressive advances should raise concern as well. This could be a sign of what's to come.

Occasionally demonstrating aggression can be considered normal but if it becomes a pattern of behavior, don't ignore it. People with aggressive behaviors often suffer from emotional issues and lack the ability to exhibit self-control. Even though I had no knowledge of this growing up, if it didn't feel right, I removed myself from the situation. When I became an adult, I did the same. Sometimes instincts are all we have, use them.

Narcissistic Behavior: Before I elaborate on narcissism, let's define the term for clarity: Narcissism can be defined as an excessive fascination with oneself to the point of completely dismissing the relevance or importance of others. This behavior can be quickly identified through conversations where the focus is solely on the individual and no one else. While conversing with this type of personality, you would be lucky to get a word in or even a thought due to your mind would be filled with what the narcissist thinks. For obvious reasons this is definitely a red flag because it demonstrates the inability to show genuine care and concern for others, which should undoubtedly be a deal breaker, but for some, this is not the case. A narcissist is only truly concerned with self and every aspect of their existence is centered on this fact. The prospect of actually having a true give and take relationship with a narcissist is relatively non-existent and in my opinion, should not be considered, but of course that is up to you.

Never anything nice to say about exes: Have you ever dated someone who talked incessantly about their exes but only in a negative manner? Didn't it make you want to ask, "If your ex was such a bad person, why did you date them or better yet, what does that say about you?" I am always leery of people like this because you should be able to say something positive about a person you spent a considerable amount of time with (*or how about not say anything at all since we all know there are two sides to every story, just a thought*).

Aside from the obvious fact that it's rude, it may also be a sign they are clearly not over the ex. If you're not totally convinced this is the case, pay close attention to how often it happens. At the very least, simply discussing why things didn't work out with the ex should be enough. Besides, the first few dates should be spent getting to know one another better, not airing "dirty laundry" of your exes. If speaking negatively about an ex is the best they can do to impress you, it says a lot about the character of the individual and just may be a reason to question whether or not you want them in your space. (*I know I get a little deep sometimes with my observations but as I stated before, I had to in order to preserve myself and it worked for me, so take it or leave it, just know that it comes from an authentic place.*)

Clarification: If your current or potential mate happens to fall into one of these categories, it does not necessarily mean they are not worthy of your time and attention, it simply means the issue needs to be addressed. If in addressing the issue, you discover valid concerns for moving on, do so without making excuses for the behavior. My intention is to help get conversations started that need to be had instead of just ignoring the elephant in the room (*to prevent the "if I only knew back then what I know now syndrome*), because some Red Flags actually turn out to be legitimate deal breakers.

26 BE YOURSELF
You Can NEVER Truly Please Others

I believe one of the greatest aspects of who I am is my insistence on being me regardless of what people say or think. Even in the awkward, unsure stage as a child, I never felt the need to be anyone other than myself because I understood that a flawed me is still better than striving to be someone I am not. People would often refer to me as "stuck-up", "snooty", "shy", "anti-social", and this mind-boggling description of " walking around like I don't need anybody", (*I guess they wanted me to need them? Huh? I am still not quite sure about this one*), at any rate, this was one of my descriptions in the eyes of others.

Admittedly, it was a source of pride for me that people couldn't quite figure me out but were quick to assign characteristics to me based merely on perceptions. This only made me more protective of myself because I firmly believe that not everyone is worthy of knowing you personally, so I would rather keep them guessing. Throughout my life I have watched individuals try desperately to fit into a mold of expectations from others, constantly chasing acceptance and validation only to end up disappointed. The bottom line is you can never truly please people; you will never be enough for everyone; you will always fall short, which is why you have to learn to be enough for you. You will drive yourself crazy trying to please others, only to find that the same people you're trying to please, are often times unhappy with who they are. Don't fall into this trap of existing to be validated by others it is definitely a lose-lose situation for you.

When I was younger, it never crossed my mind to care more about what people thought of me, than I thought of myself, however, as I grew older, I became more aware of how I contributed to the perceptions but depending on who it was, I could not have cared less. In my mind, I had to be this way to protect myself from the inevitable let down. Once again, it worked for me.

Thinking back on how I handled situations that were a threat to my individuality *(i.e. Cool Dude and T.V. Boy)*, my response was to let it go because I was unwilling to change in order to be acceptable for someone else. If my individuality becomes a problem for you, that is not my issue and therefore I will not take ownership of it. Coming to this realization at an early age helped me recognize my worth and the reasons why you don't compromise it to please others.

Find Happiness Within

At some point in my young adult life I adopted the mentality that **Happiness is Loving Yourself,** and it has become the foundation by which I live daily. I cannot recall exactly where this came from but once I began to internalize it, I often used it as a frame of reference for myself and to encourage others. My definition of what this meant was not to look for people or things to make me happy because it will not last, it cannot last because people and things come and go but I will have myself forever. When you are truly happy with yourself, people and things in and around your life have the potential to add to your happiness but not control how happy you ultimately can be. This is one mistake many people make in basing their happiness on material possessions and the people in their lives.

Please don't misunderstand my position, I love and adore my family and friends, and while they are a significant part of my life, none of them can make me happy if I am not already happy with myself. We see it everyday, people who seem to have everything: money, fame, houses, cars, relationships, friends and family, yet somehow it is not enough. Some of these same people live depressed, unfulfilled, lives and even worse, take their own lives because they cannot seem to find happiness. The inability to find happiness within can be classified in many ways, some of which are related to mental health issues (*something I am unqualified to diagnose but would be remiss if I did not acknowledge*), while others can be linked to constantly comparing oneself to unrealistic expectations from people, low self-esteem, lack of a spiritual connection and an overall sense that true happiness is a myth. In reality, happiness is what you make it and can only be gained through the realization that you ultimately control it. Stop searching for happiness in people and things, instead focus on ridding your life of negative influences that contribute to a negative outlook and make room for happiness. What better place is there to find happiness? I submit to you that at this very moment in time, there is none.

27 THE BUTTERFLY

All of the experiences and circumstances of my life have prepared me for fulfilling a purpose. I believe without them, I would not be me. I have grown to adore the person I became in spite of my flaws, in spite of my fears, in spite of the hurt, and in spite of statistics, none of which have power and authority over me.

Furthermore, I am at peace with being a fatherless child and what it meant for my upbringing and ultimately my purpose, which allows me to be free: mind, body, and soul. I am no longer bound by the uncertainties of life that sought to stifle me from growing into my purpose and moreover, I have been released from the pressures of the world that caused me to be fearful of stepping out on faith. In a nutshell, I am awesome and unapologetically me. For it is empowering to know my worth and understand the value I bring to my life and the lives of others. Coming to this realization was a journey I am grateful to have traveled and while I celebrate my individuality and purpose, I am aware there is still work to do. As long as there are people in this world who lack direction due to circumstances, who have difficulty loving self, who feel like they don't belong, who live for others, and who ultimately feel they have no purpose, I cannot rest on my laurels and give myself a pat on the back. I was freed for a purpose that is greater than me and sharing my journey is only the beginning.

Everything I have experienced up to this point demonstrates how none of us control the life we are given yet we have complete control over how we let life's circumstances define us. For every fatherless girl, there is a fatherless boy. For every fatherless boy, there is a motherless child. For every motherless child, there is one without either parent. Still, for every parentless child, there is a child who walks alone, no guardian, no family, no direction, and no love. Even those blessed to have both parents are not exempt from the trials of this world.

Life can be tough no matter how rosy or dire the circumstances and the direction, (*or lack there of*), we are provided along the way, has the power to enable us to overcome or wilt under pressure. I was empowered to be an overcomer and it is my intent to empower others in the same way. Even as I write these words, I am encouraged to achieve the impossible. When I set out on this book writing journey, I had no idea the impact my own words would have on my perspective, as I had already been molded for this moment, (*so I thought*), lending further credence to the power of self-expression. Just as journaling helped me piece my thoughts together as a child, writing this book gave me confirmation that I am presently living in the moment designed for me way back when I resisted change that would alter my life forever. It is an amazing feeling to look back over my life to see how every moment lined up perfectly imperfect yet rightfully led me to my purpose.

Many of the years I previously concluded were ambiguous, turned out to be necessary components to building a strong mental and physical foundation. Although I am unsure of how my journey will be received by others, I am confident that a purpose greater than I can imagine is upon me. I can no longer afford to remain in the background when there are so many people searching, (*as I was*), for the path of least resistance to navigate the circumstances of life. I do understand that life is ultimately what you make it, but a little direction goes a long way towards making the path clearer.

Some of the circumstances I detailed throughout this book are similar to what many people in society experience or have experienced and if my transparency can be of any assistance, it is my pleasure. While I certainly do not have all the answers, I can offer alternatives to self-defeating words and behaviors that seek to deter us from living our purpose. I encourage you today to speak life into yourself through words and in deed, with the understanding that no circumstance is greater than your purpose.

28 THE REVEAL

All of the characters I name in this book are real, yet the names were changed to protect their identities. There were many more I could have included but these characters were chosen for specific reasons, and for what it's worth, they all served a purpose. While I am not at liberty to reveal their identities, I want to be clear about the significant role each played (*even though at the time, I had no clue*).

Little Rapper Boy: He turned out to be cooler than I initially thought and we actually ended up becoming good friends and graduated from the same high school. Meeting this young man on my first day of school in a new city was exactly what I needed. His bold presence demonstrated that it is okay to be me. Even if someone else takes issue with it, the issue is theirs, not mine. Since graduating from high school, we have lost touch, but I will never forget the day we crossed paths.

Cool Dude: After graduating from middle school, I never saw Cool Dude anymore. He went to a different high school and I had little contact with him since then. We talked a few times afterward that I recall, (*on the phone*) but we were clearly not made for one another so that was perfectly fine. My encounters with Cool Dude set the stage for my independence and high self-esteem. Although I was infatuated with him, it wasn't enough to make me compromise myself for his attention. The value in this lesson was immeasurable and I am grateful for the experience.

Messy Girl/Smiley: This beautiful, intelligent young lady is still in my life today. She was the Maid of Honor in my wedding and we have built a long-lasting friendship over the past twenty-eight years that I never could have imagined, especially with the way it started. Needless to say, I took my mom's advice and kept her around as a friend and she has been an inspiration to me as well throughout my journey.

Dreamy Eyes: Well, let's just say, this young man turned out to be a not so nice person and has spent the majority of his life behind bars for murder. I never would have thought he was capable of doing the things he was convicted of, but I am forever grateful that I paid attention to that feeling of something not being quite right with him. As it turns out, it really wasn't.

Neighbor Girls: I remain friends today with these gorgeous and gifted young ladies. They were both bridesmaids in my wedding and since those days of being chased by dogs, we have stayed connected. Our children are close in age and are as close as we used to be in the old days. It is a blessing to have met them during a time when I struggled to accept my new surroundings. They could have never known what our friendship meant to me back then and I am grateful to still have them around.

Songbird: She had one of the most beautiful voices I had ever heard and although we got off to a rocky start, we grew to have mutual respect for one another. We were never close friends, (*as that was not our purpose*), but we became friendly enough to realize that we both had come to the wrong conclusions about one another. She lives in a different city so we never see each other but through this situation, I learned that people who you think are your enemies, are often times admirers who may be a little misguided in their approach. Allow time and space for forgiveness and you may actually discover a friend.

T.V. Boy: While we continued to move in the same space by way of church and high school, we were distant acquaintances with no intentions of reconciling. My time with T.V. Boy further cemented the need for self-acceptance and self-love. The fact that he chose to publicly display his lack of patience with me in the manner he did, gave me all the ammunition I needed to never turn back. Another tale of puppy love gone wrong, but ever so right as it relates to recognizing my self-worth, thus I am grateful for the experience.

Mr. Smooth: There is so much I can say about this man but let me start by saying he is still the apple of my eye. We were married in April of 2001 and I am proud that as of November 2015, we are still going strong. Yes, there have been many peaks and valleys but the love and respect we share has overcome all the valleys. Back when we were teenagers smitten with one another at the neighborhood garage party, I could not have imagined still being in love today. He has inspired me through his hard work and determination to be the best I can possibly be and there is no one else I would have wanted to travel with on this journey.

Acknowledgements

First, I thank **God** for protecting me from hurt, harm, and danger, all the days of my life, and for blessing me with a beautiful family to share it with. I could have never completed this project without your presence guiding me every step of the way. Whenever I doubted myself, you sent earth angels to encourage me to keep on going, letting me know I am on the right path.

My husband, we have essentially grown up together, experiencing all aspects of life right by each other's side. You are the real-life definition of my soul mate and I thank God for you every day. Thank you for being the man you vowed to be for me on our wedding day and for striving to be better when you fell short and I also thank you for being patient with me as I strive to be better for you. I love you.

Next, I must thank **my mother** for being an example of a good human being, with an even better heart. You taught me to speak my mind and to treat people the way I want to be treated and those lessons I have hidden in my heart. I am also thankful for your constant presence in my life, providing me with a sense of stability in the one area where you could. I am grateful for your support of my new journey and I know that I will make you proud. I love you mommy.

Of course I cannot forget **my little brother**. You have been one of my biggest supporters constantly encouraging me throughout my new journey. I remember when you walked me down the aisle and I became emotional, you told me to suck it up and keep it moving. Symbolically, this is the way I have approached obstacles in my life and you have been a huge part of my strength along the way. I love you brother.

To my **Uncle Herman**, although you may not have known, your positive words meant so much to me growing up. Your constant comparisons of me to Whitney Houston (*my idol*), and encouraging words made me feel as if I could accomplish anything. Thank you for taking the time to help me build my confidence during a sensitive time in my life, I greatly appreciate it. I love you.

To my **Pastor, Robert D. Ester**, I thank you for taking me under your wing as a daughter, providing me with a glimpse of the father I never had. Although your presence in my life was for a season, I will never forget your positive influence. You consistently encouraged me to finish my degree and to be a wise woman of God. You taught my husband and I about how to make marriage work, and to build a hedge around our relationship to prevent others from filling in the gaps. The wisdom you imparted upon me is priceless and I thank you for caring enough to share. I love you.

Kanika Randall, thank you for your undying support of my career transition and for the many words of encouragement. You have been a major piece of my support system and I am grateful that you thought enough of me to care. I completed this project on the backs of people like you. I love you.

Finally, I thank **my Dad**. Although we never had the typical father-daughter relationship, I appreciate the effort you have shown in recent years to make up for it. While we cannot rewrite the past, we can definitely reshape the future. I forgive you for not being there regardless of the reason and I am committed to moving forward because it is the right thing to do. I love you.

Inspiration

To everyone who has inspired me on this journey, thank you for using your gifts as shining examples of how to find your purpose and live it.

President Obama
Michelle Obama
Oprah Winfrey
Betty Williams
Steve Harvey
Lisa Nichols
Valerie Burton
Terri Littleton
Tisha Holman
Dr. Davin Brown
Tamika Bennett
Tyler Perry
Angel C. Knox

Bibliography

The Purpose Drive Life: What On Earth Am I here For? **– Pastor Rick Warren**

Making Great Decisions For a Life Without Limits – **Bishop T.D. Jakes**

A Daybook of Positive Thinking: Daily Affirmations of Gratitude and Happiness – **A Blue Mountain Arts Collection** (Various Contributors)

Book Cover: Tiana Cameron, Cameron Web Development,
Website: camwebdev.com
Back cover photo credit: Felicia Rosser-Johnson

About the Author

Tamara Burnett is an Author/Coach/Entrepreneur who believes in the power of loving yourself. She has spent the majority of her life as a proponent of taking personal responsibility for your happiness and not attaching levels of happiness to people and things. Although she was raised in a single-parent home, she did not allow this circumstance to dictate her value or create limitations set by others. Tamara understands that life is ultimately what you make it and therefore made every effort to carve her own path to success. After completing her degree in Communications, she grew more empowered to use her gifts to touch individuals in the world who struggle with feelings of inadequacy, and those who lack direction and purpose. Her journey began in Oakland, California and continues today in Sacramento, California where she is married with two children and intends to make an impact on society from her corner of the world.

Website: TamaraMBurnett.com
Facebook: Tamara Burnett
Instagram: Tamara M Burnett
Twitter: @MsBurnett01

38503423R00080

Made in the USA
San Bernardino, CA
07 September 2016